HALF A MAN

Sourcebooks in Negro History

HALF A MAN

THE STATUS OF THE NEGRO
IN NEW YORK

MARY WHITE OVINGTON

Foreword by Dr. Franz Boas
With a new Preface by Roy Wilkins

SCHOCKEN BOOKS · NEW YORK

TO
THE MEMORY OF MY FATHER
THEODORE TWEEDY
OVINGTON

FOREWORD

MISS OVINGTON's description of the status
of the Negro in New York City is based on
a most painstaking inquiry into his social
and economic conditions, and brings out in
the most forceful way the difficulties under
which the race is laboring, even in the large
cosmopolitan population of New York. It
is a refutation of the claims that the Negro
has equal opportunity with the whites, and
that his failure to advance more rapidly
than he has, is due to innate inability.

Many students of anthropology recognize
that no proof can be given of any material
inferiority of the Negro race; that without
doubt the bulk of the individuals composing
the race are equal in mental aptitude to
the bulk of our own people; that, although
their hereditary aptitudes may lie in slightly
different directions, it is very improbable
that the majority of individuals composing

the white race should possess greater ability
than the Negro race.

The anthropological argument is invari-
ably met by the objection that the achievements of the two races are unequal, while
their opportunities are the same. Every
demonstration of the inequality of opportunity will therefore help to dissipate
prejudices that prevent the best possible
development of a large number of our
citizens.

The Negro of our times carries even more
heavily the burden of his racial descent
than did the Jew of an earlier period; and
the intellectual and moral qualities required
to insure success to the Negro are infinitely
greater than those demanded from the white,
and will be the greater, the stricter the
segregation of the Negro community.

The strong development of racial con-
sciousness, which has been increasing during
the last century and is just beginning to
show the first signs of waning, is the gravest
obstacle to the progress of the Negro race,
as it is an obstacle to the progress of all
strongly individualized social groups. The

simple presentation of observations, like those given by Miss Ovington, may help us to overcome more quickly that self-centred attitude which can see progress only in the domination of a single type.

This investigation was carried on by Miss Ovington under the auspices of the Greenwich House Committee on Social Investigations, of which she was a Fellow.[1]

FRANZ BOAS.

---

[1] The Greenwich House Committee on Social Investigations is composed of Edwin R. A. Seligman, Chairman, Franz Boas, Edward T. Devine, Livingston Farrand, Franklin H. Giddings, Henry R. Seager, Vladimir G. Simkhovitch, Secretary.

Miss Ovington's is the second publication of the Committee, the first being Mrs. Louise Bolard More's "Wage-Earners' Budgets," published by Henry Holt & Co.

FOREWORD

CONTENTS

PREFACE
TO THE 1969 EDITION

THE YEARS covered by Mary White Ovington's *Half A Man* have been called the nadir
of American race relations. The characterization is apt and accurate. Although slavery
had its degradation and its cruelties to body
and spirit, it is a nice question as to whether
it was actually worse than the era in which so
little common humanity, to say nothing of
American citizenship rights, was delivered. In
truth, there was no forward movement. On
the contrary, there was retrogression.

In this valley of despair, the National
Association for the Advancement of Colored
People was formed by Miss Ovington and her
cofounders, William English Walling and
Henry Moskowitz. They had the help of the
liberals of the day, some sixty-odd signing the
official call to organize, which was issued on
Lincoln's Birthday 1909.

The shocking picture she described in *Half*

A Man and her organization of concerned citizens were natural reactions of Miss Ovington to the times. The Hayes–Tilden compromise of 1876 signaled that the North was washing its hands of the fortunes of the former slaves. The white South was now free to do as it chose. The Thirteenth, Fourteenth, and Fifteenth amendments to the U.S. Constitution were ignored.

In 1896 the U.S. Supreme Court, in the Plessy decision, gave its blessing to the iniquitous separate-but-equal doctrine of constitutionality which legalized both racial segregation and racial inequality in all areas of American life. The highest court steadfastly refused to rule for black Americans in any matter. Lynching, the national pastime, was not only tolerated but defended. It was symbolic of the utterly helpless position of the Negro American in the vast machinery for the administration of justice.

As for employment, the business world refused to hire Negroes, and the unions refused to admit them to membership or to apprenticeship courses. In travel in the South, only Jim Crow coaches on trains and back seats on buses were available. No dining, sleeping, or parlor cars for dark Americans. Also no accommodations in public places or in public parks and playgrounds, in theaters, hotels, and restaurants. A dismaying percentage of Northern areas had these same restrictions.

Negro applicants were barred from tax-supported universities in the South and the Border States, and strict, unpublicized quotas were in effect in the North. The per capita expenditure for the separate Negro schools in one Southern state was one-ninth the expenditure for white schools. In the rapidly building racial ghettos in Northern cities, schools were segregated administratively, rather than by law.

One of these days the white American real estate industry, its mortgage financiers and its handmaidens, the city councils and city planning boards, will have to answer for the misery squeezed mercilessly from shelter-hungry Negroes and for the extra millions in biased blood money leeched from the racially rigged housing market.

Much is made today over the election of a Negro mayor in Cleveland, but nothing is

said about the disfranchisement of tens of
millions of black Americans in past decades.
Even today, with the Voting Rights Act of
1965 in effect, only slightly more than two
million of the five million Negroes of voting
age in the South are registered to vote.

The young NAACP, of which Mary White
Ovington was a founder, addressed itself to
this appalling situation of a whole people. It
worked away at lynching, discrimination in
employment, public education, housing, voting and public accommodations, travel and
health services.

The easy branding of the NAACP effort
as out of date and the contemptuous dismissal
of the legislative and judicial processes on
which it was forced to rely stem from an
ignorance of the complete powerlessness of
the race in the period from 1909 to, say,
1935. If today's judgments are based on
today's conditions (as unequal as they still
are), they compel disparagement. If, however,
they are based upon the 1909–1935 situation,
they and the advances of 1935–1965 become
monumental.

It is not possible here to give in any detail

the history of the NAACP, one of the potent shapers of the attitudes and of the policy on race in this country. Miss Ovington sets the stage for the NAACP's great crusades. Readers of *Half A Man* may go on to study the fascinating course of race relations in America. It will be a rewarding, in many cases an eye-opening, journey but certainly one fraught with the tensions and turmoil of our past negligence and of our choices for the future.

ROY WILKINS

May, 1969

HALF A MAN

INTRODUCTION

Six years ago I met a young colored man, a college student recently returned from Germany where he had been engaged in graduate work. He was born, he told me, in one of the Gulf States, and I questioned him as to whether he intended going back to the South to teach. His answer was in the negative. "My father has attained success in his native state," he said, "but when I ceased to be a boy, he advised me to live in the North where my manhood would be respected. He himself cannot continually endure the position in which he is placed, and in the summer he comes North to be a man. No," correcting himself, "to be half a man. A Negro is wholly a man only in Europe."

Half a man! During the six years that I have been in touch with the problem of the Negro in New York this characterization has grown in significance to me. I have endeavored to know the life of the Negro as I know the life of the white American, and I have learned that while New York at times gives full recognition to his manhood, again, its race prejudice arrests his development as certainly as severe poverty arrests the development of the tenement child. Perhaps a study of this shifting attitude on the part of the dominant race, and of the Negro's reaction under it, may not be unimportant; for the color question cannot be ignored in America, nor should the position taken by her largest city be overlooked. And those who love their fellows may be glad, among New York's four millions — its Slavs and Italians, its Russians and Asiatics — to meet these dark people who speak our language and who for many generations have made this country their home.

CHAPTER I

"Up from Slavery"

The status of the Negro in New Amsterdam, a slave in a pioneer community, differed fundamentally from his position today in New York. His history from the seventeenth to the twentieth century contains many exciting incidents, but those only need be considered here that show a progress or a retardation in his attainment to manhood. What were his struggles in the past to secure his rights as a man?

Slavery in the early days of the colonies was more brutal than at the time of final emancipation. Savages recently arrived from Africa lacked the docility of blacks reared in bondage, and burning and torturing, as well as whipping, were recognized modes of punishment. Masters looked upon their Negroes, bought at the Wall Street

market from among the cargo of a recently
arrived slaver, with some suspicion and
fear. Nor were their apprehensions entirely without reason. In 1712 some of
the discontented among the New York
slaves met in an orchard in Maiden Lane
and set fire to an outhouse. Defending
themselves against the citizens who ran to
put out the flames, they fired, killing nine
men and wounding six. Retribution soon
followed. They were pursued when they
attempted flight, captured and executed —
some hanged, some burned at the stake,
some left suspended in chains to starve to
death.

Perhaps it was the memory of this small
revolt that caused the people of New York
in 1741 to lay the blame for a series of con-
flagrations upon their slaves. Nine fires
that seemed to be incendiary came one upon
another, and a robbery was committed.
To escape death herself, a worthless white
servant girl gave testimony against the
Negroes who frequented a tavern where she
was employed, declaring that a plot had
been conceived whereby the slaves would

kill all the white men and take control
of the city. New York was aflame with
fear, and evidence that at another time
would have been rejected, was listened to
by the judges with grave attention. The
slaves were allowed no defence, and before
the city had recovered from its fright, it
had burned fourteen Negroes, hanged eighteen, and transported seventy-one.[1]

Historians today think that the slaves
were in no way concerned in this so-called
"plot." The two thousand blacks in the
city might have done much mischief to the
ten thousand whites, but their servile condition made an organized movement among
them impossible. We may infer, however,
from the fear which they provoked, that
they were not all docile servants. In a
letter written at the port of New York in
1756, an English naval officer says of the
city, "The laborious people in general are
Guinea Negroes who lie under particular
restraints from the attempts they have
made to massacre the inhabitants for their

[1] Daniel Horsmanden, "New York Conspiracy, or a History of the Negro Plot."

liberty."[1] Janvier in his "Old New York"
thinks, "that the alarm bred by the so-
called Negro plot of 1741 was most effective
in checking the growth of slavery in that
city." Probably the restlessness of the slaves,
their efforts toward manhood, in a community
where there was little economic justification
for slavery, contributed to the movement
for emancipation that began in 1777.

Emancipation came gradually to the New
York Negro. Gouverneur Morris at the
state constitutional convention of 1776–1777
recommended that "the future legislature
of the state of New York take the most
effectual measures consistent with the public
safety and the private property of individuals for abolishing domestic slavery within
the same, so that in future ages every human
being who breathes the air of this state shall
enjoy the privileges of a freeman." The
postponement of action to a future legislature was keenly regretted by John Jay,
who was absent from the convention when
the slavery question arose, but who had

[1] James Grant Wilson, "History of New York," Vol. II,
p. 314.

hoped that New York might be a leader in emancipation. The state's initial measure for abolishing slavery was in 1785, when it prohibited the sale of slaves in New York. This was followed in 1799 by an act giving freedom to the children of slaves, and in 1817 by a further act providing for the abolition of slavery throughout the state in 1827. This law went into effect July 4, 1827, the emancipation day of the Negroes in New York.

With gradual emancipation and the cessation of the sale of slaves, the Negroes numerically became unimportant in the city. In 1800 they constituted ten and a half per cent of the population. Half a century later, while they had doubled their numbers, the immense influx of foreign immigrants brought their proportion down to two and seven-tenths per cent. In 1850 and 1860 their positive as well as there relative number decreased, and it was not until twenty years ago that they began to show some gain. The last census returns of 1900 give Greater New York (including Brooklyn) 60,666 Negroes in a population of 3,437,202, one and eight-tenths per cent. It seems probable that the census of 1910 will show a large positive and a slight relative Negro increase.[1]

The relative decrease in the number of Negroes did not, however, produce a decrease in the agitation upon their presence and position in the city. Their political status was a subject for heated discussion even before their complete emancipation.

[1] POPULATION OF NEW YORK FROM 1800 TO 1900:
TOTAL AND NEGRO.

BOROUGH OF MANHATTAN

	Total	Negro	Percentage of Negroes
1800	60,515	6,382	10.5
1810	96,373	9,823	10.2
1820	123,706	10,886	8.8
1830	202,589	13,976	6.9
1840	312,710	16,358	5.2
1850	515,547	13,815	2.7
1860	805,658	12,574	1.6
1870	942,292	13,072	1.5

BOROUGHS OF MANHATTAN AND BRONX

	Total	Negro	Percentage of Negroes
1880	1,206,299	19,663	1.6
1890	1,515,301	23,601	1.6
1900	2,050,600	38,616	1.9

GREATER NEW YORK

	Total	Negro	Percentage of Negroes
1900	3,437,202	60,666	1.8

The first state constitution, drafted in 1777, was without color discrimination, since it based the suffrage upon a property qualification requiring voters for governor and senators to be freeholders owning property worth £100. A Negro with such a holding was a phenomenon, a curiosity. But by 1821, when the framing of the second constitution was in progress, Negroes of some education were an appreciable element in the population, and with them ignorant, recently emancipated slaves. Should they be admitted to the full manhood suffrage contemplated for the whites? Those who favored the new democratic movement were doubtful of its applicability to colored people. Livingston, a champion of universal white manhood suffrage, was against giving the black man the vote. On the other hand, the conservative Chancellor Kent, apprehending in the new constitution "a disposition to encroach on private rights, — to disturb chartered privileges and to weaken, degrade, and overawe the administration of justice," would yet have made no color discrimination, and Peter A. Jay, who did not believe in universal white manhood suffrage, urged that colored men, natives of the country, should derive from its institutions the same privileges as white persons. The second constitution when adopted enfranchised practically all white men, but gave the Negroes a property qualification of $250. The issue of the revolution, however, was not far from men's thoughts, and "taxation without representation" was not permitted; for while no colored man might vote without a freehold estate valued at 250 dollars, *no person of color was subject to direct taxation unless he should be possessed of such real estate.*

In 1846 a third constitutional convention was held, and the same matter came up for debate. John L. Russell of St. Lawrence declared that "the Almighty had created the black man inferior to the white man," while Daniel S. Waterbury of Delaware County believed that "the argument that because a race of men is marked by a peculiarity of color and crooked hair they are not endowed with a mind equal to another class who have other peculiarities is unworthy

"UP FROM SLAVERY" 13

York City proclaimed that "We want no
masters, least of all no Negro masters. . . .
Negroes are aliens." And he predicted that
the practical effect of their admission to the
suffrage would be their exclusion from Manhattan Island. A delegation of colored men
appeared at Albany before the suffrage committee, but their arguments and those of
their friends produced no effect. The new
constitution contained the same Negro property qualification, and it was not until 1874,
after the passage of the fifteenth amendment to the Constitution of the United
States, that legislation placed the Negro
voter of New York upon the same footing
as the white.[1]

Had New York sincerely desired to keep
the Negro in an inferior position, it could
have accomplished this by refusing him an
education. This it never did, though it
suffered much tribulation regarding the place
and manner of his instruction. Before the

[1] For a full account of the Negro's political status in New
York consult Charles Z. Lincoln's "Constitutional History of
New York."

establishment of a public school system, the Manumission society, an association composed largely of Friends, though including in its membership John Jay, De Witt Clinton, and Alexander Hamilton, undertook the education of the Negro. In 1787 it opened a school for Africans on Cliff Street. One of the early teachers was Charles C. Andrews, whose little book on "The African Free Schools," published in 1830, shows a kindly tolerance for the black race. "As a result of forty years' experience," he writes, "the idea respecting the capacity of the African race to receive a respectable and even a liberal education has not been visionary." And he recites the names of some of his pupils: "Rev. Theodore S. Wright, graduate of Princeton Theological Seminary; John B. Russworm, graduate of Bowdoin; Edward Jones, graduate of Amherst; William Brown and William G. Smith, students of the medical department, Columbia College: all of them persons of color." Describing an annual exhibition of his school on May 12, 1824, he quotes from the *Commercial Advertiser* of the same date: "We never beheld a white school, of the same age (of and under the age of fifteen), in which, without exception, there was more order and neatness of dress and cleanliness of person. And the exercises were performed with a degree of promptness and accuracy which was surprising."

In 1834 the public school association took over the schools of the Manumission society, but before this time the Negroes had begun to assert themselves regarding the method and place of instruction for their children. They clamored for colored teachers and succeeded in displacing Charles Andrews himself. In 1838, at their desire, the word African was changed to colored in describing the race; but of chief importance to their educational future, they began a protest, only to end in 1900, against segregation.

Removed from the care of the Manumission society, the colored schools deteriorated. Their grade was reduced,[1] and owing to the growth of the city, their attendance was

[1] Thomas Boese's "Public Education in the City of New York," p. 227.

very irregular, the severe winter weather
often keeping children who lived at a dis-
tance at home. A Brooklyn man tells me
that, when a boy, he used to walk from his
home at East New York to Fulton Ferry,
passing inferior Brooklyn colored schools,
and after crossing the river, on up to Mulberry Street to be instructed by the popular
colored teacher, John Peterson. Here he
received a good education; but few boys
would have endured a daily trip of fourteen
miles. Increasingly parents, if the colored
school of their neighborhood was not of
the best, sent their boys and girls to be
instructed with the white boys and girls of
their district.

The state law declared that any city or
incorporated village might establish separate schools for the instruction of African
youths, provided the facilities were equal to
those of white schools, and when, in 1862,
a colored parent brought a case against the
city for forcing her child to go to a colored
school, the case was lost.[1] Nevertheless,
during the nineteenth century Negroes in

[1] King v. Gallagher, 1882.

some numbers attended white schools in both Brooklyn and New York, and Negro parents continued in their quiet but persistent efforts against segregation. Then again, New York grew too rapidly to segregate any race. The Negro boys and girls were scattered through many districts, and the attendance at colored schools fell off; in 1879 it was less than in 1878, and in 1880 less than in 1879; so that the Board of Education in 1883 decided to disestablish three colored schools.

But this involved another factor. If the colored schools were disestablished, what would become of the colored teachers? The Negroes met this issue by delaying disestablishment for a year, while the teachers went about among the parents of the ward, making friends and urging that children, *white or colored*, be sent to their schools. Numbers of new pupils of both races were brought in within the year, and at the end of the time, after a hearing before the governor, then Grover Cleveland, a bill was passed prohibiting the abolition of two of the three colored schools, but also making them open to all children regardless of color.[1]

Occasionally a colored girl graduated from the normal college of the city, but if there was no vacancy for her in the four colored schools she received no appointment. In 1896, however, a normal graduate, Miss S. E. Frazier, insisted upon her right to be appointed as teacher in any school in which there was a vacancy. She visited the ward trustees and the members of the Board of Education, and represented to them the injustice done her and her race in refusing her the chance to prove her ability as a teacher in the first school that should need a normal graduate. She was finally appointed to a position in a white school. Her success with her pupils was immediate, and since then the question of race or color has not been considered in the appointment of teachers in New York.

Until 1900, the state law permitted the establishment of separate colored schools. In that year, however, on the initiative of Theodore Roosevelt, then governor, the

[1] A. Emerson Palmer, "The New York Public School."

legislature passed a bill providing that no
person should be refused admission or be
excluded from any public school in the state
on account of race or color.[1] This closed
the question of compulsory segregation in
the state, though before this it had ceased
in New York. Public education was thus
democratized for the New York Negroes,
their persistent efforts bringing at the end
complete success.

While the colored people in New York
started with segregated schools and attained
to mixed schools, the movement in the
churches was the reverse. At first the
Negroes were attendants of white churches,
sitting in the gallery or on the rear seats,
and waiting until the white people were
through before partaking of the communion;
but as their number increased they chafed
under their position. Why should they be
placed apart to hear the doctrine of Christ,
and why, too, should they not have full
opportunity to preach that doctrine? The
desire for self-expression was perhaps the
greatest factor in leading them to separate

Laws of New York, Chapter 492.

from the white church. In 1796 about
thirty Negroes, under the leadership of
James Varick,[1] withdrew from the John
Street Methodist Episcopal Church, and
formed the first colored church of New York.
Varick had been denied a license to preach,
but now as pastor of his own people, he
was recognized by the whites and helped
by some of them. He was the founder
of the African Methodist Episcopal Zion
Church.

The Abyssinian Baptist Church was organized in 1800 by a few colored members who
withdrew from the First Baptist Church,
then in Gold Street, to establish themselves
on Worth Street,[2] and in 1818 the colored
Episcopalians organized St. Philip's Church.
In 1820 one of their race, Peter Williams,
for six years deacon, became their preacher.

Another prominent church was the colored Congregational, situated, in 1854, on
Sixth Street; and it was the determined
effort of its woman organist to reach the
church in time to perform her part in the

[1] B. F. Wheeler, D.D., "The Varick Family."
[2] Geo. H. Hansell, "Reminiscences of New York Baptists."

Sunday morning service that led to an important Negro advance in citizenship.

In the middle of the last century the right of the Negro to ride in car or omnibus depended on the sufferance of driver, conductor, and passenger. Sometimes a car stopped at a Negro's signal, again the driver whipped up his horses, while the conductor yelled to the "nigger" to wait for the next car. Entrance might always be effected if in the company of a white person, and the small child of a kindly white household would be delegated to accompany the homeward bound black visitor into her car where, after a few minutes, conductor and passengers having become accustomed to her presence, the young protector might slip away. Such a situation was very galling to the self-respecting negro.

In July, 1854, Elizabeth Jennings, a colored school-teacher and organist at the Congregational Church, attempted to board a Third Avenue car at Pearl and Chatham Streets. She was hurrying to reach the church to perform her part in the service. The conductor stopped, but as Miss Jen-

nings mounted the platform, he told her that
she must wait for the next car, which was
reserved for her people. "I have no people,"
Miss Jennings said. "I wish to go to church
as I have for six months past, and I do not
wish to be detained." The altercation continued until the car behind came up, and the
driver there declaring that he had less room
than the car in front, the woman was grudg-
ingly allowed to enter the car. "Remember," the conductor said, "if any passenger
objects, you shall go out, whether or no, or
I'll put you out."

"I am a respectable person, born and
brought up in New York," said Miss Jennings, "and I was never insulted so before."

This again aroused the conductor. "I
was born in Ireland," he said, "and you've
got to get out of this car."

He attempted to drag her out. The woman
clung to the window, the conductor called
in the driver to help him, and together they
dragged and pulled and at last threw her
into the street. Badly hurt, she nevertheless jumped back into the car. The driver
galloped his horses down the street, passing

every one until a policeman was found who pushed the woman out, not, however, until she had taken the number of the car. She then made her way home.

Elizabeth Jennings took the case into court, and it came before the Supreme Court of the State in February, 1855, Chester A. Arthur, afterwards President of the United States, being one of the lawyers for the plaintiff. The judge's charge was clear on the point that common carriers were bound to carry all respectable people, white or colored, and the plaintiff was given $225 damages, to which the court added ten per cent and costs; and to quote the New York *Tribune's* comment on the case,[1] "Railroads, steamboats, omnibuses, and ferryboats will be admonished from this as to the rights of respectable colored people." [2]

When you talk with the elderly educated colored people of New York today, they tell you that before the War were "dark days." The responsibility felt by the thoughtful

[1] *New York Tribune*, February 23, 1855.
[2] "The Story of an Old Wrong," in *The American Woman's Journal*, July, 1895.

Negroes was very great. They had not only
their own battles to wage, but there were
the fugitives who were entering the city
by the Underground Railroad, whom they
must assist though it cost them their own
liberty. In 1835 a Vigilance Committee
was formed in New York City to take charge
of all escaping slaves, and also to prevent
the arrest and return to slavery of free men
of color. Colored men served on this Committee, and its secretary was the minister
of the church to which Elizabeth Jennings
was endeavoring to make her way that
Sunday morning, the Reverend Charles B.
Ray. In 1850 the New York State Vigilance Committee was formed with Gerritt
Smith as President and Ray as Secretary.
Ray's home was frequently used to shelter
fugitives.[1] Once a young man, stepping up
to the door and learning that it was Charles
Ray's house, whistled to his companions in
the darkness, and fourteen black men made
their appearance and received shelter. There
would also come the task of negotiating for
the purchase of a slave, or this proving

[1] Life of the Reverend Charles B. Ray.

impossible, for the careful working out of a means for his escape. Dark days, indeed, but made memorable to the Negro by heroic work and the friendship of great men. Perhaps the two races have never worked together in such fine companionship as at the unlawful and thrilling task of protecting and aiding the fugitive.

The hardest year of the century for the Negro was 1863, when the draft riot imperilled every dark face. Many Negroes fled from the city. Colored homes were fired, the Orphan Asylum for colored children on Fifth Avenue was burned, and even the dead might not be buried save at the peril of undertaker and priest. Elizabeth Jennings, now Mrs. Graham, lost a child when the rioting was at its height. An undertaker named Winterbottom, a white man, was brave enough to give his services, winning the lasting gratitude and patronage of the colored people. With the danger of violence about them, the father and mother went to Greenwood Cemetery, where the Reverend Morgan Dix of Trinity Church read the burial service at the grave.

With the end of the War and the passage of the fourteenth and fifteenth amendments came a revulsion of feeling for the race. "I remember," an old time friend of the Negro tells me, "when the fifteenth amendment was passed. The colored people stood in great numbers on the streets, and on their faces was a look of gratitude and thanksgiving that I shall never forget." Following the amendment came the State Civil Rights Bill in 1873, declaring that all persons should be entitled to full and equal accommodations in all public places; and discrimination for a time largely ceased.

While the colored people were winning citizenship, their progress in industry was also considerable. Until 1860 the race was infrequently segregated, and black and white were neighbors, not only in their homes, but in business. Samuel R. Scottron, a careful Negro writer, compiled a long list of the trades in which Negroes engaged before the War. Besides the various lines of domestic service, in which they were more frequently seen than today — coachmen, cooks, waitresses, seamstresses, barbers —

there were many craftsmen, ship-builders, trimmers, riggers, coopers, caulkers, printers, tailors, carpenters. "Second-hand clothing shops were everywhere kept by colored men. All the caterers and restaurant keepers of the high order, as well as small places, were kept by colored men. . . . Varick and Peters kept about the most pretentious barber shop in the city. Patrick Reason was one of the most capable engravers. The greatest among the restaurateurs was Thomas Downing, who kept a restaurant under what is now the Drexel Building, corner of Wall and Broad Streets. The drug stores of Dr. James McCune Smith on West Broadway, and Dr. Philip A. White on Frankfort Street, were not outclassed by any kept by white men in their day." [1]

And so the list goes on. It is perhaps somewhat exaggerated in the importance in the city's business life which it gives to the colored race. Charles Andrews, in 1837, says of the pupil who graduates from his school, "He leaves with every avenue closed against him — doomed to encounter as much

[1] *Colored American Magazine*, October, 1907.

prejudice and contempt as if he were not
only destitute of that education which dis-
tinguishes the civilized from the savage, but
as if he were incapable of receiving it."
And he goes on to tell of those few who have
been able to learn trades, and their subse-
quent difficulties in finding employment in
good shops. White journeymen object to
working in the same shop with them, and
many of the best lads go to sea or become
waiters, barbers, coachmen, servants, laborers. But he is writing of an early date,
and the opinion of the colored people seems
to be that, before our large foreign immigration, the Negro was more needed in New
York than today and received a large share
of satisfactory employment. His chief competitor was the Irish immigrant, like himself an agricultural laborer, without previous
training in business, and he was frequently
able to hold his own in his shop. His long
experience in domestic service, moreover,
made him a better caterer than the repre-
sentatives of any other nationality that had
yet entered the city. His churches were
flourishing, thus securing a profession for

which he had natural ability, and as we have
seen, colored men and women taught in the
New York schools.

The city grew rapidly after 1875, and the
colored society, the little group that had
attained to modest means and education,
bought homes, chiefly in Brooklyn, where
land was easier to secure than in Manhattan,
and strove to enlarge the opportunities for
those who were to come after them. Color
prejudice had waned, and they often met
with especial consideration because of their
race. Had they been white they would
have slipped into the population and been
lost, as happened to the Germans and the
Irish, who had been their competitors. As
it was, they formed a society apart from the
rest of the city, meeting it occasionally in
work or through the friendship of children,
who, left to themselves, know no race.
They had battled against prejudice and had
won their rights as citizens.

As we look at the life of a segregated
people, however, we see that we tend always
to regard not the individual but the group.
The Negro is a man in Europe, because

there he is an individual, standing or falling by his own merits. But in America, even in so cosmopolitan a city as New York, he is judged, not by his own achievements, but by the achievements of every other New York black man. So we will leave these able colored Americans, who won much both for themselves and for their race, and turn to the mass of the Negroes, the toiling poor, who dwell in our tenements today.

CHAPTER II

WHERE THE NEGRO LIVES

IT is thirty-five years since, in his Symphony, Sidney Lanier told of

> "The poor
> That stand by the inward opening door
> Trade's hand doth tighten evermore,
> And sigh their monstrous foul air sigh
> For the outside hills of liberty."

Were Lanier writing this today, we should wonder whether New York's crowded tenements had not served as inspiration for his figure. The island of Manhattan, about eight miles long by two miles wide, with an additional slender triangle of five miles at the north end, in 1905, housed two million one hundred and twelve thousand people. These men and women and children were not scattered uniformly throughout the island, but were placed in selected corners, one thousand to the acre, while a mile or so away large comfortable homes held families of two or three. This was Manhattan's condition in 1905, and with each succeeding year more congestion takes place, and more pressure is felt upon the inward opening door.[1]

The Negro with the rest of the poor of New York has his part in this excessive overcrowding. The slaver in which he made his entrance to this land provided in floor space six feet by one-foot-four for a man, five feet by one-foot-four for a woman, and four feet by one-foot-four for a child.[2] This outdoes any overcrowding New York can produce, but an ever increasing cost in food and rent is bringing into her interior bedrooms a mass of humanity approximating that of the slaver's ship. These new-comers, however, are not unwilling occupants, since unlike the slaves they may spend their day and much of their night amid an ocean of changing and exciting incidents. If you are young and strong, you care less where you sleep, than where you may spend your waking hours.

[1] Harold M. Finley in *Federation*, May, 1908.
[2] Thomas Clarkson, "History of the Abolition of the Slave Trade," p. 378.

From among the millions of New York's poor, can we pick out the Negroes in their tenements? This is not so difficult a task as it would have proved fifty years ago when the colored were scattered throughout the city; today we find them confined to fairly definite quarters. A black face on the lower East Side is viewed with astonishment, while on the middle West Side it is no more noticeable than it would be in Atlanta or New Orleans. Roughly we may count five Negro neighborhoods in Manhattan: Greenwich Village, the middle West Side, San Juan Hill, the upper East, and the upper West sides. Brooklyn has a large Negro population, but it is more widely distributed and less easily located than that of Manhattan.

Of the five Manhattan neighborhoods the oldest is Greenwich Village, according to Janvier once the most attractive part of New York, where the streets "have a tendency to sidle away from each other and to take sudden and unreasonable turns." Here one finds such fascinating names as Minetta Lane and Carmine and Cornelia Streets.

These and neighboring thoroughfares grow daily more grimy, however, and no longer merit Janvier's praise for cleanliness, moral and physical. The picturesque, friendly old houses are giving way to factories with high, monotonous fronts, where foreigners work who crowd the ward and destroy its former American aspect.

Among the old time aristocracy bearing Knickerbocker names there are a few colored people who delight in talking of the fine families and past wealth of old Greenwich Village. Scornful of the gibberish-speaking Italians, they sigh, too, at their own race as they see it, for the ambitious Negro has moved uptown, leaving this section largely to widowed and deserted women and degenerates. The once handsome houses, altered to accommodate many families, are rotten and unwholesome, while the newer tenements of West Third Street are darkened by the elevated road, and shelter vice that knows no race. Altogether, this is not a neighborhood to attract the new-comer. Here alone in New York I have found the majority of the adults northern born, men and women

who, unsuccessful in their struggle with city
life, have been left behind in these old forgotten streets.[1]

The second section, north of the first, lies
between West Fourteenth and West Fifty-
ninth Streets, and Sixth Avenue and the
Hudson River. In 1880 this was the centre
of the Negro population, but business has
entered some of the streets, the Pennsyl-
vania Railroad has scooped out acres for its
terminal, and while the colored houses do

[1] Place of birth of 1036 New York Negro tenement dwellers.
These figures were obtained chiefly from personal visits:

	Totals	East Side	Green-wich Village	Middle West Side	San Juan Hill	Upper West Side
New England	18	1	4	7	5	1
West	11	1	0	5	4	1
New York............	157	6	47	42	55	7
New Jersey...........	18	1	4	3	9	1
Pennsylvania	19	0	3	3	12	1
Maryland	37	1	0	6	27	3
District of Columbia ...	26	0	1	5	16	4
Virginia	375	8	15	71	244	37
Carolinas.............	217	6	16	64	127	4
Gulf States	65	0	2	23	39	1
Canada	2	0	1	1	0	0
West Indies	87	1	6	13	67	0
Europe	4	0	1	0	3	0
	1036	25	100	243	608	60

not diminish in number, they show no decided increase. No one street is given over
to the Negro, but a row of two or three or
six or even eight tenements shelter the black
man. The shelter afforded is poorer than
that given the white resident whose dwelling
touches the black, the rents are a little
higher, and the landlord fails to pay attention to ragged paper, or to a ceiling which
scatters plaster flakes upon the floor. In
the Thirties there are rear tenements reached
by narrow alley-ways. Crimes are committed by black neighbor against black
neighbor, and the entrance to the rear yard
offers a tempting place for a girl to linger at
night. A rear tenement is New York's only
approach to the alley of cities farther south.

There are startling and happy surprises in
all tenement neighborhoods, and I recall
turning one afternoon from a dark yard
into a large beautiful room. Muslin cur-
tains concealed the windows, the brass bed
was covered with a thick white counterpane,
and on either side of the fireplace, where
coal burned brightly in an open grate, were
two rare engravings. It was a workroom,

and the mistress of the house, steady, capable, and very black, was at her ironing-board. By her sat the colored mammy of the story book rocking lazily in her chair. She explained to me that her daughter had found her down south, two years ago, and brought her to this northern home, where she had nothing to do, for her daughter could make fifty dollars a month. This home picture was made lastingly memorable by the younger woman's telling me softly as she went with me to the door, "I was sold from my mother, down in Georgia, when I was two years old. I ain't sure she's my mother. *She* thinks so; but I can't ever be sure."

Homes beautiful both in appearance and in spirit can rarely occur where people must dwell in great poverty, but there are many efforts at attractive family life on these streets. A few of the blocks are orderly and quiet. Thirty-seventh Street, between Eighth and Ninth Avenues, is largely given over to the colored and is rough and noisy. Here and down by the river at Hell's Kitchen the rioting in 1900 between the Irish and the Negro took place. Men are ready for a

fight today, and the children see much of
hard drinking and quick blows.

"The poorer the family, the lower is the
quarter in which it must live, and the more
enviable appears the fortune of the anti-
social class." [1] A vicious world dwells in
these streets and makes notorious this section
of New York. For this is a part of the
Tenderloin district, and at night, after the
children's cries have ceased, and the fathers
and mothers who have worked hard during
the day have put out their lights, the auto-
mobiles rush swiftly past, bearing the men
of the "superior race." Temptation is continuous, and the child that grows up pure
in thought and deed does so in spite of his
surroundings.

Before reaching West Fifty-ninth Street,
the beginning of our third district, we come
upon a Negro block at West Fifty-third
Street. When years ago the elevated railroad was erected on this fashionable street,
white people began to sell out and rent to
Negroes; and today you find here three
colored hotels, the colored Young Men's and

[1] S. N. Patten, "New Basis of Civilization," p. 52.

Young Women's Christian Associations, the offices of many colored doctors and lawyers, and three large beautiful colored churches. The din of the elevated drowns alike the doctor's voice and his patient's, the client's and the preacher's.

From Fifty-ninth Street, walking north on Tenth Avenue, we begin to ascend a hill that grows in steepness until we reach Sixty-second Street. The avenue is lined with small stores kept by Italians and Germans, but to the left the streets, sloping rapidly to the Hudson River, are filled with tenements, huge double deckers, built to within ten feet of the rear of the twenty-five foot lot, accommodating four families on each of the five floors. We can count four hundred and seventy-nine homes on one side of the street alone!

This is our third district, San Juan Hill, so called by an on-looker who saw the policemen charging up during one of the once common race fights. It is a bit of Africa, as Negroid in aspect as any district you are likely to visit in the South. A large majority of its residents are Southerners and

West Indians, and it presents an interesting study of the Negro poor in a large northern city. The block on Sixtieth Street has some white residents, but the blocks on Sixty-first, Sixty-second, and Sixty-third are given over entirely to colored. On the square made by the north side of Sixty-first, the south side of Sixty-second Streets, and Tenth and West End Avenues, 5.4 acres, the state census of 1905 showed 6173 inhabitants.[1] All but a few of these must have been Negroes, as the avenue sides of the block, occupied by whites, are short and with low houses. It is the long line of five-story tenements, running eight hundred feet down the two streets, that brings up the enumeration. The dwellings on Sixty-first and Sixty-second Streets are human hives, honeycombed with little rooms thick with human beings. Bedrooms open into air shafts that admit no

[1] Some doubt is cast upon this figure. The New York Health Department in an enumeration of its own, in 1905, found a population of 3833. There is no question, however, of the great congestion of this block and the one north and south of it. The erection of new tenements has gone on rapidly since 1905, sweeping away the children's playgrounds, and making this one of the most crowded centres of New York.

fresh breezes, only foul air carrying too often
the germs of disease.

The people on the hill are known for their
rough behavior, their readiness to fight, their
coarse talk.   Vice is abroad, not in insidious
form as in the more well-to-do neighborhood
farther north, but open and cheap.   Boys
play at craps unmolested, gambling is preva-
lent, and Negro loafers hang about the street
corners and largely support the Tenth Avenue
saloons.

But San Juan Hill has many respectable
families, and within the past five years it has
taken a decided turn for the better.   The
improvement has been chiefly upon Sixty-
third Street where two model tenements, one
holding one hundred, the other one hundred
and sixty-one families, have been opened
under the management of the City and
Suburban Homes Company, the larger one
having been erected by Mr. Henry Phipps.
Planning for a four per cent return on their
investment, these landlords have rented only
to respectable families, and their rule has
changed the character of the block.[1]   Old

[1] Too much cannot be said of the beneficial effect of good

houses have been remodelled to compete with
the newer dwellings, street rows have ceased,
and the police captain of the district, we are
told, now counts this as one of the peaceful
and law-abiding blocks of the city. When
its other blocks show a like improvement,
San Juan Hill will no longer merit its belligerent name.

The lower East Side of Manhattan, a many-
storied mass of tenements and workshops,
where immigrants labor and sleep in their
tiny crowded rooms, was once a fashionable
American district. At that time Negroes
dwelt near the whites as barbers, caterers,
and coachmen, as laundresses and waiting-
maids. But with the removal of the people
whom they served, the colored men and

housing in a colored neighborhood, when under such able
management as the City and Suburban Homes Company.
Decent homes under competent management are absolutely
necessary to an improvement in the Negro quarters of Manhattan and of Brooklyn as well. I can speak with some
authority of the good done by the Phipps houses on West
Sixty-third Street, as I lived, for eight months, the only white
tenant in the one hundred and sixty-one apartments. Church
and philanthropy had done and are doing excellent work on
these blocks, but a sudden and marked improvement came
from good housing, from the building of clean, healthful
homes for law-abiding people.

women left also, and it is difficult to find an
African face among the hundreds of thousands of Europeans south of Fourteenth
Street. On Pell Street, in the Chinese quarter, there used to be two colored families on
friendly terms with their neighbors, who,
however, went uptown for their pleasures
and their church.

It is not until we reach Third Avenue and
Forty-third Street that we come to the East
Side Negro tenement. From this point,
such houses run, a straggling line, chiefly
between Second and Third Avenues, to the
Bronx where the more well-to-do among the
colored live. At Ninety-seventh Street, and
on up to One Hundredth Street, dark faces
are numerous. About six hundred and fifty
Negro families live on these four streets and
around the corner on Third Avenue. Occasionally they live in houses occupied by
Jews or Italians. Above this section there
are a number of Negro tenements in the One
Hundred and Thirties, between Madison
and Fifth Avenues — almost a West Side
neighborhood, since it adjoins the large
colored quarter to the west of Fifth Avenue.

On the whole, the East Side is not often sought by the colored as a place of residence. Their important churches are in another part of the city, and every New Yorker knows the difficulty in making a way across Central Park. Yet, the neighborhood is not uncivil to them, and one rarely reads here of race friction. Doubtless this is in part owing to the smallness of the population, all of Manhattan east of Fifth Avenue containing but fourteen per cent of the apartments occupied by colored in the city; but it is partly, too, that Jews and Italians prove less belligerent tenement neighbors than Irish.

Five years ago, those of us who were interested in the Negro poor continually heard of their difficulty in securing a place to live. Not only were they unable to rent in neighborhoods suitable for respectable men and women, but dispossession, caused perhaps by the inroad of business, meant a despairing hunt for any home at all. People clung to miserable dwellings, where no improvements had been made for years, thankful to have a roof to shelter them. Yet all the time new-law tenements were being built, and Gentile

and Jew were leaving their former apartments
in haste to get into these more attractive
dwellings. At length the Negro got his
chance; not a very good one, but something
better than New York had yet offered him
— a chance to follow into the houses left
vacant by the white tenants. Owing in part
to the energy of Negro real estate agents, in
part to rapid building operations, desirable
streets, near the subway and the elevated
railroad, were thrown open to the colored.
This Negro quarter, the last we have to note
and the newest, has been created in the past
eight years. When the Tenement House
Department tabulated the 1900 census figures for the Borough of Manhattan, and
showed the nationalities and races on each
block, it found only 300 colored families in
a neighborhood that today accommodates
4473 colored families.[1] This large increase
is on six streets, West Ninety-ninth, between
Eighth and Ninth Avenues, West One Hundred and Nineteenth, between Seventh and
Eighth Avenues, and West One Hundred and

[1] The Tenement House Department tabulated the number
of Negro families living in tenements on these streets. I have
counted the number of flats rented to colored people.

Thirty-third to One Hundred and Thirty-
sixth Streets, between Fifth and Seventh
Avenues, with a few houses between Seventh
and Eighth, and on Lenox Avenues. There
are colored tenements north and south of
this; and while these figures are correct
today,[1] they may be wrong tomorrow, for
new tenements are continually given over to
the Negro people. Moreover, on all of these
streets are colored boarding and lodging
houses, crowded with humanity. Houses
today fall into the hands of the Negro as a
child's blocks, placed on end, tumble when
a push is given to the first in the line. The
New York *Times*, in August, 1905, gives a
graphic account of the entrance of the
colored tenant on West Ninety-ninth Street.
Two houses had been opened for a short time
to Negroes when the other house-owners
capitulated, and the colored influx came:
"The street was so choked with vehicles
Saturday that some of the drivers had to
wait with their teams around the corners for
an opportunity to get into it. A constant
stream of furniture trucks loaded with the

[1] July 15, 1910.

household effects of a new colony of colored
people who are invading the choice locality
is pouring into the street. Another equally
long procession, moving in the other direction, is carrying away the household goods
of the whites from their homes of years."
The movement is not always so swift as this,
but it is continuous.

This last colored neighborhood perhaps
ought not to be spoken of as belonging to the
poor; not to Lanier's poor whose door pressed
so tighteningly inward. Here are homes
where it is possible, with sufficient money,
to live in privacy, and with the comforts of
steam heat and a private bath. But rents
are high, and if money is scarce, the apartment must be crowded and privacy lost.
Moreover, vice has made its way into these
newly acquired streets. The sporting class
will always pay more and demand fewer
improvements than the workers, and, unable
to protect himself, the respectable tenant
finds his children forced to live in close
propinquity to viciousness. Each of these
new streets has this objectionable element in
its population, for while some agents make

earnest efforts to keep the property they handle respectable, they find the owner wants money more than respectability.

In our walk up and down Manhattan, turning aside and searching for Negro-tenanted streets, we ought to see one thing with clearness — that the majority of the colored population live on a comparatively few blocks. This is a new and important feature of their New York life, and in certain parts of the city it develops a color problem, for while you seem an inappreciable quantity when you constitute two per cent of the population in the borough, you are of importance when you form one hundred per cent of the population of your street. This congestion is accompanied by a segregation of the race. The dwellers in these tenements are largely new-comers, men and women from the South and the West Indies,[1] seeking the North for greater freedom and for economic opportunity. Like any other

[1] The yearly arrivals of "African blacks" at the port of New York, secured from the Immigration Commissioner, are as follows: 1902–03, 110; 1903–04, 547; 1904–05, 1189; 1905–06, 1757; 1906–07, 2054; 1907–08, 1820; 1908–09, 2119. The year runs from July 1 to June 30.

strangers they are glad to make their home
among familiar faces, and they settle in the
already crowded places on the West Side.
Freedom to live on the East Side next door
to a Bohemian family may be very well, but
sociability is better. The housewife who timidly hangs her clothes on the roof her first
Monday morning in New York is pleased
to find the next line swinging with the laundry of a Richmond acquaintance, who in-
structs her in the perplexing housekeeping
devices of her flat. No chattering foreigner
could do that. And while to be welcome in
a white church is inspiring, to find the girl
you knew at home, in the next pew to you, is
still more delightful when you have arrived,
tired and homesick, at the great city of New
York. So the colored working people, like
the Italians and Jews and other nationalities,
have their quarter in which they live very
much by themselves, paying little attention
to their white neighbors. If the white
people of the city have forced this upon
them, they have easily accepted it. Should
this two per cent of the population be compelled to distribute itself mathematically

over the city, each ward and street having its
correct quota, it would evince dissatisfaction. This is not true of the well-to-do
element, but of the mass of the Negro
workers whose homes we have been visiting.
Loving sociability, these new-comers to the
city — and it is in the most segregated districts that the greater number of southern
and British born Negroes are found — keep
to their own streets and live to themselves.
If they occupy all the sidewalk as they talk
over important matters in front of their
church, the outsider passing should recognize
that he is an intruder and take to the curb.
He would leave the sidewalk entirely were
he on Hester Street or Mulberry Bend.
New-comers to New York usually segregate,
and the Negro is no exception.

While congestion and segregation seem
important to us as we look at these colored
quarters, I suspect that the matter most
pertinent to the Negro new-comer is, not
where he will live nor how he will live, but
whether he will be able to live in New York
at all, whether he can meet the landlord's
agent the day he comes to the door. For

New York rents have mounted upwards as have her tenements. The Phipps model houses, built especially to benefit the poor, charge twenty-five dollars a month for four tiny rooms and bath; and while this is a little more than the dark old time rooms would bring, it takes about all of the twenty-five dollars you make running an elevator, to get a flat in New York. What wonder that, once secured, it is overrun with lodgers, or that, if privacy is maintained, there is not enough money left to feed and clothe the growing household. The once familiar song of the colored comedian still rings true in New York:

"Rufus Rastus Johnson Brown,
What you gwine ter do when de rent comes roun'?"

CHAPTER III

THE CHILD OF THE TENEMENT

WITHIN the last few years white Americans, many of whom were formerly ignorant of their condition, have been taught that they are possessed of a racial antipathy for human beings whose color is not their own. They have a "natural contrariety," "a dislike that seems constitutional" toward the dark tint that they see on another's face. But however well they may have conned their lesson, it breaks down or is likely to be forgotten in the presence of a Negro baby; for a healthy colored baby is a subject, not for natural contrariety, but for sympathetic cuddling. They are most engaging newcomers, these "delicate bronze statuettes," [1] only warm with life, and smiling good will upon their world.

Not many colored babies are born in New York, at least not enough to keep pace with

[1] Dudley Kidd's, "Savage Childhood," a delightful book.

the deaths. The year 1908 saw in all the boroughs 1973 births as against 2212 deaths at all ages.[1]

In this same year the colored births for Manhattan and the Bronx were 1459, and the deaths under one year of age 424, an infant mortality rate of 290 to every thousand.[2] That is, two babies in every seven died under one year of age. The white infant mortality rate was 127.7, a little less than half that of the colored.

Why should we have in New York this enormous colored infant death rate? Many physicians believe it indicates a lack of physical stamina in the Negro, an inability to resist disease. This may be so, but before falling back upon race as an explanation of high infant mortality, we need to exhaust other possible causes. We do not question the vitality of the white race when we read

[1] Report of the Department of Health, City of New York, 1908, pp. 844, 849. The returns for births, the report states, are incomplete.

[2] This per cent is obtained from two sources, the births from the Department of Health report, and the deaths from the Mortality Statistics of the United States Census, 1908. "Colored" includes Chinese, a negligible quantity in the infant population.

that in parts of Russia 500 babies out of every thousand die within the year; nor do we believe the people of Fall River, a factory town in Massachusetts, have an inherent inability to resist disease, though their infant mortality rate in 1900 was 260 in one thousand births. We look in these latter cases, as we should in the former, to see if we find those conditions which careful students of the subject tell us accompany a high infant death rate.

Among the first of the accepted causes of infant mortality is the overcrowding of cities. We have viewed overcrowding as a usual condition among the Negroes of New York, and have seen the small, ill-ventilated bedroom where the baby spends much of its life. Heat, with its accompanying growth of bacteria and swift process of decomposition, is a second cause. New York's high infant mortality comes in the summer months when in the poorest quarters it has been known to reach four hundred in the thousand.[1] In the hot, crowded

[1] Third Annual Report of the New York Milk Committee, 1909.

tenements, and no place can be so hot as New York in one of its July record-breaking weeks, the babies die like flies, and yet not like flies, for the flies buzz in hundreds about the little hot faces. Excitement, late hours, constant restlessness, these, too, cause infant mortality. On a city block tenanted by hundreds of men and women and little children, no hour of the night is free from some disturbance. Children whimper as they wake from the heat, babies cry shrilly, and the brightly-lighted streets are rarely without the sound of human footsteps. The sensitive new-born organism knows nothing of the quiet and restful darkness of nature's night.

But the most important cause of infant mortality [1] is improper infant feeding. And here we meet with a condition that confronts the Negro babies of New York far more than it confronts the white. For a properly fed baby is a breast fed baby, or else one whose food has been prepared with great care, and mothers forced by necessity to go

[1] See G. Newman, "Infant Mortality," for a careful study of this whole subject.

out to work, cannot themselves give their babies this proper food. It is among the infants of mothers at work that mortality is high. Mr. G. Newman, an English authority on this subject, gives an interesting example of this in Lancashire, where, during the American civil war, many of the cotton operatives were out of employment and many more worked only half time. Privation was great. A quarter of the mill hands were in receipt of poor relief, the general death rate increased, but *the infant mortality rate decreased.* The mothers, forced by circumstances to remain away from the factory, though in a state of semi-starvation, by their nursing and by their care of the home preserved the lives of their infants. Negro mothers, owing to the low wage earned by their husbands, for the general welfare of the family and to avoid semi-starvation, like the Lancashire women, leave their homes, but they thereby sacrifice the lives of many of their babies. The percentage for 1900 of Negro married women in New York engaging in self-supporting work was 31.4 in every hundred; of white married women 4.2 in

every hundred, seven times as many in proportion among the Negroes as among the
whites.[1] The Negro also shows a large percentage of widows, a quarter of all the female
population over ten years of age. Some of
these, we have no means of knowing how
many, are widows only in name, and have
babies for whom they must in some way pro-
vide support. The colored mother who has
no husband often takes a position in domestic
service and boards her baby, paying usually
by the month, and finding the opportunity
to visit her infant perhaps once a week.
Sometimes she secures a "baby tender" who
can give kindly, intelligent care; but under
the best conditions her child will be bottle
fed and in tenement surroundings inimical
to health, while sometimes the woman to
whom she intrusts her infant will be ignorant of the simplest matters of hygiene.

I remember an old colored woman, she
must be dead by this time, who kept a baby
farm. Her health was poor, and when I
saw her, she had taken to her bed and lay

[1] Census, 1900, combination of Population table and
Women at Work.

in a dark room with two infants at her side.
They were indescribably puny, with sunken
cheeks and skinny arms and hands, weigh-
ing what a normal child should weigh at
birth, and yet six and seven months old.
The woman talked to me enthusiastically
of salvation and gave filthy bottles to her
charges. She was exceptionally incompe-
tent, but there are others doing her work,
too old or too ignorant properly to attend
to the babies under their care.

Mothers who go out to day's-work are
also unable to nurse their babies or to pre-
pare all their food. The infant is placed
in the care of some neighbor or of a growing
daughter, who may be the impatient "little
mother" of a number of charges. When the
hot summer comes, such a baby is likely to
fall the victim of epidemic diarrhœa, caused
by pollution of the milk. Newman has a
striking chart of infant death rates in Paris
in which he pictures a rate mounting in
one week as high as 256 in the thousand
among the artificially fed infants, while for
the same week, among the breast fed babies,
the mortality is 32. The Negro mother,

seeking self-support by keeping clean another's house or caring for another's children, finds her own offspring swiftly taken
from her by a disease that only her nourish-
ing care could forestall.[1]

Remedial measures have for some time
been taken in New York to check infant
mortality, and they have met with some
success. The distribution of pasteurized
milk by Mr. Nathan Straus, the establishment of milk stations during the summer
months in New York and Brooklyn where
mothers at slight cost may secure proper
infant food, and where much educative
work is done by the visiting nurse, the mul-
tiplication of day nurseries, all these have
helped to decrease the death rate. The
Negroes have been benefited by these remedial agencies, but their percentage of 290
is still a matter for grave attention.

Two out of seven of New York's Negro
babies die in the first year, but the other
five grow up, some with puny arms and

[1] It is interesting to see that the married women of Fall
River, where we found a very high infant death rate, show
a percentage of married women at work of twenty in a
hundred.

ricketty legs, others again too hardy for
bad food or bad air to harm.

Like the babies these children suffer from
their mother's absence at work. Family
ties are loose, and more than other children
they are handicapped by lack of proper
home care. In an examination of the records of the Children's Court for three years
I found that out of 717 arraignments of
colored children, 221 were for improper
guardianship, 30.8 per cent of the whole.
Among the Russian children of the East
Side, Tenth and Eleventh Wards, only
15 per cent of arraignments were on this
complaint, indicating twice as many children
without parental care among the colored
as among the children of the Tenth and
Eleventh Wards. Rough colored girls, also,
whose habits were too depraved to permit of
their remaining without restraint, were frequently committed to reformatories.

Truancy is not uncommon in colored
neighborhoods, though few cases come before
the courts. Sometimes the boy or girl is
kept at home to care for the younger children, but again, lacking the mother's over-

sight, he remains on the street when he should be in school, or arrives late with ill prepared lessons.

Asking a teacher of long experience among colored and white children concerning their respective scholarship, he assured me that the colored child could do as well as the white, but didn't. "From 20 to 50 per cent of the mothers of my colored children," he said, "go out to work. There is no one to oversee the child's tasks, and consequently little conscientious study."

One can scarcely blame the children; and certainly one cannot blame the mothers for toiling for their support. And the fathers, though they work faithfully, are rarely able to earn enough unaided to support their families. Perhaps in time the city may improve matters by opening its school-rooms for a study period in the afternoon.

But meanwhile the children are without proper care. This is not hard to endure in the summer, but in winter it is very trying to be without a home. Poor little cold boys and girls, some of them mere babies! You see them in the late afternoon sitting

on the tenement stairs, waiting for the long
day to be done. It seems a week since
they were inside eating their breakfast.
The city has not pauperized them with a
luncheon, and they have had only cold food
since morning. Sometimes they have been
all day without nourishment. When the
door is opened at last, there are many help-
ful things for them to do for their mother,
and reading and arithmetic are relegated
to so late an hour that their problem is
only temporarily solved by sleep.

Not all the colored working women, however, go out for employment. Laundry
work is an important home industry, and
one may watch many mothers at their
tubs or ironing-boards from Monday morning until Saturday night. This makes the
tenement rooms, tiny enough at best, sadly
cluttered, but it does not deprive the children of the presence of their mother, who
accepts a smaller income to remain at home
with them. For after we have made full
allowance for the lessening of family ties
among the Negroes by social and economic
pressure, we find that the majority of the

colored boys and girls receive a due share of proper parental oversight. They are fed on appetizing food, cleanly and prettily dressed, they are encouraged to study and to improve their position, and they are given all the advantages that it is possible for their mothers and fathers to secure.

Jack London tells in the "Children of the Abyss" of the East Side of London, where "they have dens and lairs into which to crawl for sleeping purposes, and that is all. One can not travesty the word by calling such dens and lairs 'homes.'" I have seen thousands of Negro dwelling-places, but I cannot think of half a dozen, however great their poverty, where this description would be correct. No matter how dingy the tenement, or how long the hours of work, the mother, and the father, too, try to make the "four walls and a ceiling" to which they return, home. Visitors among the New York poor, in the past and in the present, testify that given the same income or lack of income, the colored do not allow their surroundings to become so cheerless or so filthy as the white, and that when there is an opportunity for the mother to spend some time in the house, the rooms take on an air of pleasant refinement. Pictures decorate the walls, the sideboard contains many pretty dishes, and the table is set three times a day. Meals are not eaten out of the paper bag common on New York's East Side, but there is something of formality about the dinner, and good table manners are taught the children. The tenement dwelling becomes a home, and the boys and girls pass a happy childhood in it.

Watching the colored children for many months in their play and work, I have looked for possible distinctive traits. The second generation of New Yorkers greatly resembles the "Young America" of all nationalities of the city, shrill-voiced, disrespectful, easily diverted, whether at work or at play, shrewd, alert, and mischievous — the New York street child. I remember once helping with a club of eight boys where seven nationalities were represented, and where no one could have distinguished Irish from German or Jew from Italian, with his eyes shut. Had a Negro been brought up among them he would quickly have taken on their ways. Of the colored children who model their lives after their mischievous young white neighbors, many outdo the whites in depravity and lawlessness; but among the boys and girls who live by themselves, as on San Juan Hill, one sees occasional interesting traits.

The records of the Children's Court of New York (Boroughs of Manhattan and the Bronx) throw a little light on this matter, and are sufficiently important to quote with some fulness. For the three years studied, 1904, 1905, 1906, I tabulated the cases of the colored children brought before the court, and also the cases of the children of the Tenth and Eleventh Wards, chiefly Hungarians and Russian Jews, expecting to find, in two such dissimilar groups, interesting comparisons. The following table shows the result of this study. The court in its annual report gives the figures for the total number of arrests which I have incorporated in my table:

RECORD OF ARRESTS IN CHILDREN'S COURT OF MANHATTAN
AND THE BRONX FOR 1904, 1905, 1906

	Negro Arrests		10th and 11th Wards Arrests		Total arrests for all children in Manhattan and Bronx	
	No. of children	Arrests per cent	No. of children	Arrests per cent	No. of children	Arrests per cent
Petit larceny	56	7.8	139	6.8	2,697	10.1
Grand larceny	27	3.8	108	5.3	878	3.3
Burglary — Robbery .	27	3.8	116	5.7	1,383	5.2
Assault	27	3.8	61	3.0	669	2.5
Improper guardianship	221	30.8	305	15.0	6,386	23.9
Disorderly child — un-governable child ...	90	12.6	124	6.1	1,980	7.4
Depraved girl	33	4.6	21	1.1	312	1.2
Violation of labor law.	0	0	73	3.5	592	2.1
Unlicensed peddling [1] .	0	0	130	6.4	0	.0
Truancy	5	.7	23	1.0	298	1.1
Malicious mischief....	1	.1	9	.4	179	.7
Violation of Park Corporation ordinances.	0	0	25	1.2	175	.7
Mischief, including craps, throwing stones, building bonfires, fighting, etc....	214	29.8	896	43.7	10,267	38.4
Unclassified felonies, misdemeanors......	13	1.8	16	.7	799	3.0
All others	3	.4	3	.1	90	.4
	717	100.0	2049	100.0	26,705	100.0

Percentage of Negro to total, 1904–1907 ....2.7
Percentage of Negro to total, 1907–1910 ....1.9

[1] My tabulations of the Negro and Tenth and Eleventh
Ward Children are from the Court's unpublished records to

Our table shows us that which we have already noted, the high percentage of improper guardianship among the Negroes and the grave number of depraved Negro girls. For the sins of petit larceny, grand larceny, and burglary, putting the three together, the colored child shows a slightly smaller percentage than the East Side white, a noticeably smaller percentage than the total number of children. The sin of theft is often swiftly attributed to a black face, but this percentage indicates that the colored child has no "innate tendency" to steal. Ten per cent of the arrests among the East Side children are for unlicensed peddling and violation of the labor law, but no little Negro boys plunge into the business world before their time. They have no keen commercial sense to lead them to undertake transactions on their own account, and they are not desired by purchasers of boy labor in the city.

The most important heading, numerically,

which I was allowed access. The absence of any figures for Unlicensed Peddling in the Total indicates that in its printed reports the Court has included Unlicensed Peddling with Unclassified Misdemeanors.

is that of mischief, and here the Negro falls far behind the Eastsider, behind the average for the whole. While depravity among the girls and improper guardianship are the race's most serious defects, as shown by the arrests among its children in New York, tractability and a decent regard for law are among its merits. The colored child, especially if he is in a segregated neighborhood, is not greatly inclined to mischief. My own experience has shown me that life in a tenement on San Juan Hill is devoid of the ingenious, exasperating deviltry of an Irish or German-American neighborhood. No daily summons calls one to the door only to hear wildly scurrying footsteps on the stairs. Mail boxes are left solely for the postman's use, and hallways are not defaced by obscene writing. There is plenty of crap shooting, rarely interfered with by the police, but there is little impertinent annoyance or destructiveness.

An observer, watching the little colored boys and girls as they play on the city streets, finds much that is attractive and pleasant. They sing their songs, learned at school and

on the playground, fly their kites, spin their
tops, run their races. They usually finish
what they begin, not turning at the first
interruption to take up something else.
They move more deliberately than most
children, and their voices are slower to adopt
the New York screech than those of their
Irish neighbors on the block above them.
Altogether they are attractive children,
particularly the smaller ones, who are more
energetic than their big brothers and sisters. Good manners are often evident.
While receiving an afternoon call from two
girls, aged four and five, I was invited by
the older to partake of half a peanut, the
other half of which she split in two and gen-
erously shared with her companion. "Gim'
me five cents," I once heard a Negro boy of
twelve say to his mother who walked past
him on the street. She did not seem to
hear, but the boy's companion, a youth of
the same age, reproved him severely for
his rude speech. When walking with an
Irish friend, who had worked among the
children of her own race, I saw a colored
boy run swiftly up the block to meet his

mother. He kissed her, took her bundle
from her, and carrying it under his arm,
walked quietly by her side to their home.
"There are many boys here," I said, "who
are just as courteous as that." "Is that
so?" she retorted quickly, "Then you
needn't be explaining to me any further
the reason for the high death rate."

The gentle, chivalrous affection of the
child for its mother is daily to be seen among
these boys and girls. "Your African," said
Mary Kingsley, "is little better than a
slave to his mother, whom he loves with a
love he gives to none other. This love of
his mother is so dominant a factor in his
life that it must be taken into consideration in attempting to understand the true
Negro."[1] And if the child lavishes affection upon its parent, the mother in turn
gives untiringly to her child. She is the
"mammy" of whom we have so often heard,
but with her loving care bestowed, as it
should be, upon her own offspring. She
tries to keep her child clean in body and spirit
and to train it to be gentle and good; and

[1] Mary Kingsley, "West African Studies," p. 319.

in return usually she receives a stanch devotion. I once found fault with a colored girl of ten years for her rude behavior with her girl companions, adding that perhaps she did not know any better, at which she turned on me almost fiercely and said, "It's our fault; we know better. Our mothers learn us. It's we that's bold." As one watches the boys and girls walking quietly up the street of a Sunday afternoon to their Sunday-school, neatly and cleanly dressed, one appreciates the anxious, maternal care that strives as best it knows how, to rear honest and God-fearing men and women.

Paul Lawrence Dunbar has painted the Negro father, his "little brown baby wif sparklin' eyes," nestling close in his arms. Working at unusual hours, the colored man often has a part of the day to give to his family, and one sees him wheeling the baby in its carriage, or playing with the older boys and girls.

Negroes seem naturally a gentle, loving people. As you live with them and watch them in their homes, you find some coarseness, but little real brutality. Rarely does a father or mother strike a child. Travellers in Central and West Africa describe them as the most friendly of savage folk, and where, as in our city, they live largely to themselves, they keep something of these characteristics. But it is only a step in New York from Africa into Italy or Ireland; and the step may bring a sad jostling to native friendliness. To hold his own with his white companions on the street or in school, the Negro must become pugnacious, callous to insult, ready to hit back when affronted. Many are like the little girl who told me that she did not care to play with white children, "because," she explained, "my mother tells me to smack any one who calls me nigger, and I ain't looking for trouble." The colored children aren't looking for trouble. They have a tendency to run away from it if they see it in the form of a gang of boys coming to them around the corner. They believe if they had a fight, it wouldn't be a fair one, and that if the policeman came, he would arrest them and not their Irish enemies. So they grow up on streets through which few white men pass, leading their own lives with their own people and thinking not overmuch of the other race that surrounds them.   But the day comes when school is over, and the outside world, however indifferent they may be to it, must be met.   They must go out and grapple with it for the means to hire a cooking stove and a dark bedroom of their own; they must think of making money.   So they stand at the corner of their street, looking out, and then move slowly on to find what opportunity is theirs to come to a full manhood. The way ahead does not seem very bright, and some move so timidly that failure is sure to meet them at the first turning.   But some have the courage of the little colored girl, aged four, who led a line of kindergarten children up their street and then on to the unknown country that lay between them and Central Park.   At the first block a mob of Irish boys fell upon them, running between the lines, throwing sticks, and calling "nigger" with screams and jeers. The leader held her head high, paying no attention to her persecutors.   She neither

quickened nor slowed her pace, and when
the child at her side fell back, she pulled her
hand and said, "Don't notice them. Walk
straight ahead."

CHAPTER IV

EARNING A LIVING — MANUAL LABOR AND
THE TRADES

IN "The American Race Problem," one of
our recent important books upon the Negro,
the author, Mr. Alfred Holt Stone of Mississippi, after a survey of the world, declares
that "to me, it seems the plainest fact con-
fronting the Negro is that there is but one
area of any size wherein his race may obey
the command to eat its bread in the sweat of
its face side by side with the white man.
That area is composed of the Southern
United States." [1]

On examination we find that only men of
English and North European stock are
"white" to Mr. Stone, and that his statement is too sweeping by a continent or two,
but as applying to the United States, it will

[1] Alfred Holt Stone, "Studies in the American Race Problem," p. 164.

75

usually meet with unqualified approval. It is generally believed that discrimination continually retards the Negro in his search for employment in the North, while in the South "he is given a man's chance in the commercial world." Northern men visiting southern colored industrial schools advise the pupils to remain where they are, and restless spirits among the race are assured that it is better to submit to some personal oppression than to go to a land of uncertain employment. The past glory of the North is dwelt upon, its days of black waiters, and barbers, and coachmen, but the present is painted in harsh colors.

There is some truth in this comparison of economic conditions among the Negroes in the North and in the South, but it must not be taken too literally. Today's tendency to minimize southern and maximize northern race difficulties, while strengthening the bonds between white Americans, sometimes obscures the real issues regarding colored labor in this country. We need to look carefully at conditions in numbers of selected localities, and we can find no northern city more worthy of our study than New York.

The New York Negro constitutes today but two per cent of the population of Manhattan, one and eight-tenths per cent of that of Greater New York; and, as many workers in Manhattan live in Brooklyn, the larger area is the better one to consider. In 1900, the census volume on occupations gives the number of males over ten years of age engaged in gainful occupations in Greater New York at 1,102,471, and of that number 20,395 or 1.8 per cent, eighteen in every thousand, are Negroes. In Atlanta, to take a southern commercial centre, 351 out of every thousand male workers are Negroes. This enormous difference in the proportion of colored workers to white must never be forgotten in considering the labor situation North and South. We cannot expect in the North to see the Negro monopolizing an industry which demands a larger share of workers than he can produce, nor need we admit that he has lost an occupation when he does not control it.

We often come upon such a statement as

that of Samuel R. Scottron, a colored business man, who, writing in 1905, said, "The Italian, Sicilian, Greek, occupy quite every industry that was confessedly the Negro's forty years ago. They have the bootblack stands, the news stands, barbers' shops, waiters' situations, restaurants, janitorships, catering business, stevedoring, steamboat work, and other situations occupied by Negroes."[1] Did the colored men have all this forty years ago when they were only one and a half per cent of the population? If so, there were giants in those days, or New York was much simpler in its habits than now. At present the control by the colored people of any such an array of industries would be quite impossible. To take four out of the nine occupations enumerated: the census of 1900 gives the number of waiters at 31,211; barbers, 12,022; janitors, 6184; bootblacks, 2648; a total of 52,065. But in 1900 there were only 20,395 Negro males engaged in gainful occupations in New York. Without a vigorous astral body the 20,000-odd colored men could not occupy half these

[1] New York *Age*, August 24, 1905.

jobs. If they dominated in the field of
waiters they must abandon handling the
razor, and not all the colored boys could
muster 2684 strong to black the boots of
Greater New York. We must at the outset
recognize that as a labor factor the Negro in
New York is insignificant.

The volume of the federal census for 1900
on occupations shows us how the Negroes
are employed in New York City. There are
five occupational divisions, and the Negroes
and whites are divided among them as
follows:

	White	Per cent	Negro	Per cent
Agricultural pursuits........	9,853	.9	251	1.2
Professional service	60,037	5.6	729	3.6
Domestic and personal service	189,282	17.6	11,843	58.1
Trade and transportation....	398,997	37.1	5,798	28.4
Manufacturing and mechanical pursuits..............	417,634	38.8	1,774	8.7
Total................	1,075,803	100.0	20,395	100.0

But in examining in detail the occupations
under these different headings, we get a
clearer view of the place the Negro main-
tains as a laborer by finding out how many

workers he supplies to every thousand workers in a given occupation. He should average eighteen if he is to occupy the same economic status as the white man. Taking the first (numerically) important division, Domestic and Personal Service, we get the following table:

DOMESTIC AND PERSONAL SERVICE

	Total number of males in each occupation.	Number of Negroes in each occupation.	Number of Negroes to each 1000 workers in occupation.
Barbers and hairdressers	12,022	215	18
Bootblacks..................	2,648	51	20
Launderers	6,881	70	10
Servants and waiters	31,211	6,280	201
Stewards	1,366	140	103
Nurses	1,342	22	16
Boarding and lodging house keepers	474	10	21
Hotel keepers	3,139	23	7
Restaurant keepers	2,869	116	40
Saloon keepers and bartenders..	17,656	111	6
Janitors and sextons	6,184	800	129
Watchmen, firemen, policemen..	16,093	116	7
Soldiers, sailors, marines	3,707	56	15
Laborers (including elevator tenders, laborers in coal yards, longshoremen, and stevedores)	98,531	3,719	38
Total, including some occupations not specified	206,215	11,843	57

The most important of these groups, not only in absolute numbers, but in proportion to the whole working population, is the servants and waiters. Two hundred out of every thousand (we must remember that the proportion to the population would be eighteen out of every thousand) are holding positions with which they have long been identified in America. We cannot tell from the census how many "live out," or how many are able to go nightly to their homes, how many have good jobs, and how many are in second and third rate places. A study of my own of 716 colored men helps to answer one of these questions. Out of 176 men coming under the servants' and waiters' classification, I found 5 caterers, 24 cooks, 26 butlers, 30 general utility men, 41 hotel men, and 50 waiters. Sixty per cent of the 176 lived in their own homes, not in their masters'. Some of the cooks and waiters were on Pullman trains or on river boats or steamers; only a few were in first-class positions in New York. In the summer many of these men are likely to go to country hotels, and with the winter, if New York

offers nothing, migrate to Palm Beach or
stand on the street corner while their wives
go out to wash and scrub.[1] "An' it don't
do fer me ter complain," one of them tells
me, "else he gits 'high' an' goes off fer good."
Waiters in restaurants sometimes do not
make more than six dollars a week, to be
supplemented by tips, bringing the sum up
to nine or ten dollars. Hall men make about

[1] Occupations in 1907 of 716 colored men (secured from
records of the Young Men's Christian Association and personal visits) compared with census figures of occupations in
1900.

	716 Men	Census
Agricultural pursuits......................	—	1.2
Professional service, 27 men...............	3.8	3.6
Domestic and personal service, 363 men	50.6	58.1
5 barbers, 5 caterers, 24 cooks, 30 general util-ity men, 41 hotel men, 76 waiters and butlers, 8 valets, 35 janitors and sextons, 29 long-shoremen, 5 laborers in tunnels, 7 asphalt workers, 57 elevator men, 41 laborers.		
Trade and transportation, 279 men.........	39.0	28.4
10 chauffeurs, 35 drivers, 13 expressmen, 8 hostlers, 12 messengers, 14 municipal em-ployees, 127 porters in stores, 15 porters on trains, 24 clerks, 21 merchants.		
Manufacturing and mechanical pursuits, 47 men....................................	6.6	8.7
	100.0	100.0

the same, but both waiters and hall men in clubs and hotels receive large sums in tips or in Christmas money. The Pullman car waiters have small wages but large fees.

Looking again at the census, we see that 129 out of every thousand janitors and sextons are colored. The janitor's position varies from the impecunious place in a tenement, where the only wage is the rent, to the charge of a large office or apartment building. Then come the laborers, nearly four thousand strong, with the elevator boy as a familiar figure. Forty per cent of the 139 laborers in my own tabulation were elevator boys, for, except in office buildings and large stores and hotels, this occupation is given over to the Negro, who spends twelve hours a day drowsing in a corner or standing to turn a wheel. Paul Lawrence Dunbar wrote poetry while he ran an elevator, and ambitious if less talented colored boys today study civil service examinations in their unoccupied time; but the situation as a life job is not alluring. Twenty-five dollars a month for wage, with perhaps a half this sum in tips, twelve hours on duty, one week in the night

time and the next in the day — no wonder
the personnel of this staff changes frequently
in an apartment house. A bright boy will
be taken by some business man for a better
job, and a lazy one drifts away to look for
an easier task, or is dismissed by an irate
janitor.

Quite another group of laborers are the
longshoremen who, far from lounging indo-
lently in a hallway, are straining every
muscle as they heave some great crate into
a ship's hold. The work of the New York
dockers has been admirably described by
Mr. Ernest Poole, who says of the thirty
thousand longshoremen on the wharves of
New York — Italians, Germans, Negroes,
and Swedes, "Far from being the drunkards
and bums that some people think them, they
are like the men of the lumber camps come
to town — huge of limb and tough of muscle,
hard-swearing, quick-fisted, big of heart."
Their tasks are heavy and irregular. When
the ship comes in, the average stretch of
work for a gang is from twelve to twenty
hours, and sometimes men go to a second
gang and labor thirty-five hours without

sleep. Their pay for this dangerous, exhausting toil averages eleven dollars a week. "There are thousands of Negroes on the docks of New York," Mr. Poole writes me, "and they must be able to work long hours at a stretch or they would not have their jobs." At dusk, Brooklynites see these black, huge-muscled men, many of them West Indians, walking up the hill at Montague Street. In New York they live among the Irish in "Hell's Kitchen" and on San Juan Hill. They are usually steady supporters of families.

New York demands strong, unskilled laborers. To some she pays a large wage, and Negroes have gone in numbers into the excavations under the rivers, though a lingering death may prove the end of their two and a half or perhaps six or seven dollar a day job. Many colored men worked in the subway during its construction. One sees them often employed at rock-drilling or clearing land for new buildings. About a third of the asphalt workers, making their two dollars and a half a day, are colored. Some educated, refined Negroes choose the laborer's work rather than pleasanter but poorly paid occupations. A highly trained colored man, a shipping clerk, making seven dollars a week, left his employer to take a job of concreting in the subway at $1.80 a day. His decision was in favor of dirty, severe labor, but a living wage.

When the next census is published, those of us who are carefully watching the economic condition of the Negro expect to find a movement from domestic service into the positions of laborers, including the porters in stores, who belong in our second census division.

Kelly Miller[1] describes the massive buildings and sky-seeking structures of our northern city, and finds no status for the Negro above the cellar floor. One can see the colored youth gazing wistfully through the office window at the clerk, whose business reaches across the ocean to bewilderingly wonderful continents, knowing as he does that the employment he may find in that office will be emptying the white man's waste paper basket.

[1] Kelly Miller, *Radicals and Conservatives; and Other Essays on the Negro in America,* New York: Schocken Books, 1968, p. 143. (Originally published as *Race Adjustment,* 1908, p. 129.)

TRADE AND TRANSPORTATION

	Total number of males in each occupation.	Number of Negroes in each occupation.	Number of Negroes to each 1000 workers in occupation.
Agents — commercial travellers	27,456	67	2
Bankers, brokers, and officials of banks and companies........	11,472	7	0
Bookkeepers — accountants ...	22,613	33	1
Clerks, copyists (including shipping clerks, letter and mail carriers)......................	80,564	423	5
Merchants (wholesale and retail)	72,684	162	2
Salesmen	45,740	94	2
Typewriters	3,225	36	11
Boatmen and sailors	8,188	145	18
Foremen and overseers	3,111	18	6
Draymen, hackmen, teamsters..	51,063	1439	28
Hostlers	5,891	633	107
Livery stable keepers..........	967	9	9
Steam railway employees	11,831	70	6
Street railway employees	7,375	11	1
Telegraph and telephone operators......................	2,430	6	2
Hucksters and peddlers	12,635	69	5
Messengers, errand and office boys	13,451	335	25
Porters and helpers (in stores, etc.)	11,322	2143	188
Undertakers	1,572	15	9
Total, including some occupations not specified	405,675	5798	14

This, however, does not apply to government positions, and a large number of the 423 colored clerks in 1900 were probably in United States and municipal service. The latter we shall consider later as we study the Negro and the municipality. Of the former, in 1909 there were about 176 in the New York post-offices.[1] Ambitious boys work industriously at civil service examinations, and a British West Indian will even become an American citizen for the chance of a congenial occupation. The clerkship, that to a white man is only a stepping-stone, to a Negro is a highly coveted position.

I have made two divisions of this census list; the first includes those occupations requiring intellectual skill and carrying with them some social position, the second, those demanding only manual work. It is in the second that the colored man finds a place, and as a porter he numbers 2143, and reaches almost as high a percentage as the waiter and servant. Porters' positions are paid from five to fifteen dollars a week, the man

[1] It is difficult to get accurate figures as no official record is kept of color.

receiving the latter wage performing also the duties of shipping clerk. There is some opportunity for advance, always within the basement, and there are regular hours and a fairly steady job.

The heading of draymen, hackmen, and teamsters, with 28 colored in every thousand, shows that the Negro has not lost his place as a driver. The chauffeur does not appear in the census, but the Negro is steadily increasing in numbers in this occupation, and conducts three garages of his own.

The last census division to be considered in this chapter is that of Manufacturing and Mechanical Pursuits.

When Mr. Stone wrote of the Southern States as the only place in which the Negro could "earn his bread in the sweat of his face," side by side with the white man, he must especially have been thinking of workers in the skilled trades. Unskilled laborers in New York are drenched in a common grimy fellowship. But in this last division the Negro is conspicuous by his absence. Only four in every thousand where there should be eighteen! In Atlanta, under this

MANUFACTURING AND MECHANICAL PURSUITS

	Total number of males in each occupation.	Number of Negroes in each occupation.	Number of Negroes to each 1000 workers in occupation.
Engineers, firemen (not locomotive)	16,579	227	14
Masons (brick and stone)	12,913	94	7
Painters, glaziers, and varnishers	27,135	177	6
Plasterers	4,019	51	12
Blacksmiths.................	7,289	29	4
Butchers	12,643	31	2
Carpenters and joiners	29,904	94	3
Iron and steel workers.........	10,372	40	4
Paper hangers	962	18	19
Photographers...............	1,590	22	14
Plumbers, gas and steam fitters.	16,614	31	2
Printers, lithographers, and pressmen......................	21,521	53	2
Tailors	56,094	69	1
Tobacco and cigar factory operators	11,689	189	16
Fishermen and oystermen......	1,439	65	45
Miners and quarrymen	326	21	64
Machinists	17,241	47	3
Total, including some occupations not specified	419,594	1774	4

Bakers, boot and shoe makers, gold and silver workers, brass workers, tin plate and tin ware makers, box makers, cabinet makers, marble and stone cutters, book-binders, clock and watch makers, confectioners, engravers, glass workers, hat and cap makers, and others — not more than nineteen in any one occupation, nor a higher per cent than four in a thousand.

division, the race reaches almost its due
proportion, 279 in a thousand instead of 351.
The largest number in any trade in New
York is 189 men among the Cuban tobacco
workers. Seventy-five per cent of all the
masons in Atlanta are colored men, while in
New York the colored are less than one
per cent. Looking down the list we see that
the figures are small and the percentage insignificant. The highly skilled and best paid
trades are seemingly as far removed from
the Negro as the positions of floor-walkers
or cashiers of banks.

Omitting for the present the professional
class, we have reviewed the Negro as a
worker, and neither in wages nor choice of
occupation has he risen far to success. In
domestic service he has gone a little down
the ladder, serving in less desirable positions
than in former years. Why has this happened? What good reasons are there for
these conditions?

The first and most obvious reason is race
prejudice. No display of talent, however
prodigious, will open certain occupations to
the colored race. As a salesman he could

teach courteous manners to some of our white salesmen in New York, but he is never given a chance. There are a few Negroes, digging in the tunnels or sweeping down the subway stairs, who are capable of filling the clerkships that are counted the perquisites of the whites; but clerkships are only accessible as they are associated with municipal or federal service. Of course there are exceptions, and though they do not affect the rule, they show the existence of a few employers who ignore the color line, and a few Negroes of inexhaustible perseverance.

Mr. Stone argues that the Negro in the South profits by the strict drawing of the color line, since the white man, always considered the superior, is not lowered in the eyes of the community by working with the black man. The Southern white may lay bricks on the same wall with the Southern black, secure in his superior social position. But this seems fanciful as an explanation of labor conditions. The black doctor, for instance, in those localities where the color line is most rigid, may not ask the white doctor to consult with him; or if he does, his prompt removal from the community is requested. Colored postal clerks are in disfavor in the South, though not colored postmen. North or South, *the Negro gets an opportunity to work where he is imperatively needed.* Constituting one-third of the working population, he can make a place for himself in the laboring world of Atlanta as he cannot in New York. Pick up the 20,000 New York Negroes and drop them in Liberia, and in two or three weeks Ellis Island could empty out sufficient men to fill their places; but remove a third of the male workers from Atlanta, and the city for years would suffer from the calamity. If they are the only available source of labor, colored men can work by the side of white men; but where the white man strongly dominates the labor situation, he tries to push his black brother into the jobs for which he does not care to compete.

We have seen, however, that in some occupations in New York the Negroes appear in such proportion as should be sufficient to secure them excellent positions; the most conspicuous instance being that of the 200 colored waiters out of every thousand. Why, then, do we not see Negroes serving in the best hotels the city affords?

It has been an ideal of American democracy, a part of its strenuous individualism, that each member of the community should have full liberty in the pursuit of wealth. The ambitious, capable boy who walks barefooted into the city, and at the end of twenty years has outdistanced his country schoolmates, becoming a multi-millionaire while they are still farm drudges, is the example of American opportunity. But this ability to separate one's self from the rest of one's fellows and attain individual greatness is rarely possible to a segregated race. In domestic service individual colored men have shown ambition and high capability, but they have never been able to get away from their fellows like the country boy — to leave the farm drudges and take a place among the most proficient of their profession. They must always work in a race group. And this Negro group is like the small college that tries to win at football against a competitor with four times the number of students and

a better coach. The two hundred colored
waiters, competing against the eight hundred
white ones, lose in the game and are given a
second place, which the best must accept
with the worst. When, then, we criticize a
capable colored man for failing to keep a
superior position we must remember that
he is tied to his group and has little chance
of advancement on his individual merit.

The census division of mechanical pursuits shows only a few colored men working at
trades, and the paucity of the numbers is often
attributed by the Negro to a third obstacle
in the way of his progress, the trade-union.

To the colored man who has overcome race
prejudice sufficiently to be taken into a shop
with white workmen, the walking delegate
who appears and asks for his union card
seems little short of diabolical; and all the
advantages that collective bargaining has
secured, the higher wage and shorter working-
day, are forgotten by him. I have heard
the most distinguished of Negro educators,
listening to such an incident as this, declare
that he should like to see every labor union
in America destroyed. But unionism has

come to stay, and the colored man who is asked for his card had better at once get to work and endeavor to secure it. Many have done this already, and organized labor in New York, its leaders tell us, receives an increasing number of colored workmen. Miss Helen Tucker, in a careful study of Negro craftsmen in the West Sixties,[1] found among 121 men who had worked at their trades in the city, 32, or 26 per cent in organized labor. The majority of these had joined in New York. Eight men, out of the 121, had applied for entrance to unions and not been admitted. This does not seem a discouraging number, though we do not know whether the other 81 could have been organized or not. Many, probably, were not sufficiently competent workmen. In 1910, according to the best information that I could secure, there were 1358 colored men in the New York unions. Eighty of these were in the building trades, 165 were cigar makers, 400 were teamsters, 350 asphalt workers, and 240 rock-drillers and tool sharpeners.[2]

[1] *Southern Workman*, October, 1907, to March, 1908.
[2] See foot-note on opposite page.

Entrance to some of the local organizations is more easily secured than to others, for the trade-union, while part of a federation, is autonomous, or nearly so. In some

[2] In 1906, and again in 1910, I secured a counting of the New York colored men in organized labor. The lists run as follows:

	1906	1910
Asphalt workers	320	350
Teamsters	300	400
Rock-drillers and tool sharpeners.	250	240
Cigar makers	121	165
Bricklayers	90	21
Waiters	90	not obtainable
Carpenters	60	40
Plasterers	45	19
Double drum hoisters	30	37
Safety and portable engineers	26	35
Eccentric firemen	15	0
Letter carriers	10	30
Pressmen	10	not obtainable
Printers	6	8
Butchers	3	3
Lathers	3	7
Painters	3	not obtainable
Coopers	1	2
Sheet metal workers	1	1
Rockmen	1	not obtainable
Total	1385	1358

The large number of bricklayers in 1906 is questioned by the man, himself a bricklayer, who made the second counting. However, the number greatly decreased in 1908 when the stagnation in business compelled many men to seek work in other cities.

of the highly skilled trades,. to which few
colored men have the necessary ability to
demand access, the Negro is likely to be
refused, while the less intelligent and well-
paid forms of labor press a union card upon
him. Again, strong organizations in the
South, as the bricklayers, send men North
with union membership, who easily transfer
to New York locals. Miss Tucker finds the
carpenters', masons', and plasterers' organizations easy for the Negro to enter. There
is in New York a colored local, the only
colored local in the city, among a few of the
carpenters, with regular representation in
the Central Federated Union. The American Federation of Labor in 1881 declared
that "the working people must unite irre-
spective of creed, color, sex, nationality, or
politics." This cry is for self-protection, and
where the Negroes have numbers and ability
in a trade, their organization becomes important to the white. It may be fairly said
of labor organization in New York that it
finds and is at times unable to destroy race
prejudice, but that it does not create it.[1]

[1] The comment of the Negro bricklayer who secured my

A fourth obstacle, and a very important one, is the lack of opportunity for the colored boy. The only trade that he can easily learn is that of stationary engineer, an occupation at which the Negroes do very well. Colored boys in small numbers are attending evening trade schools, but their chance of securing positions on graduation will be small. The Negro youth who is not talented enough to enter a profession, and who cannot get into

figures is important. "A Negro," he says, "has to be extra fit in his trade to retain his membership, as the eyes of all the other workers are watching every opportunity to disqualify him, thereby compelling a superefficiency. Yet at all times he is the last to come and the first to go on the job, necessitating his seeking other work for a living, and keeping up his card being but a matter of sentiment. While all the skilled trades seem willing to accept the Negro with his travelling card, yet there are some which utterly refuse him; for instance, the house smiths and bridge men who will not recognize him at all. While membership in the union is necessary to work, yet the hardest part of the battle is to secure employment. In some instances intercession has been made by various organizations interested in his industrial progress for employment at the offices of various companies, and favorable answers are given, but hostile foremen with discretionary power carry out their instructions in such a manner as to render his employment of such short duration that he is very little benefited. Of course, there are some contractors who are very friendly to a few men, and whenever any work is done by them, they are certain of employment. Unfortunately, these are too few."

the city or government service, has slight opportunity. Nothing is so discouraging in the outlook in New York as the crowding out of colored boys from congenial remunerative work.

The last obstacle in the way of the Negro's advancement into higher occupations is his inefficiency. Race prejudice denies him the opportunity to prove his ability in many occupations, and the same spirit forces him to work in a race group; but the colored men themselves are often unfitted for any labor other than that they undertake.

The picture that is sometimes drawn of many thousands of highly skilled Southern colored men forced in New York to give up their trades and to turn to menial labor is not a correct one. Richard R. Wright, Jr., who has made a careful study of the Negro in Philadelphia,[1] finds that the majority of colored men who come to that city are from the class of unskilled city laborers and country hands; the minority are the more skilful artisans and farmers and domes-

---

[1] R. R. Wright, Jr.'s "Migration of Negroes to the North," Annals of the American Academy, May, 1906.

tic servants, with a number also of the vagrant and criminal classes.

In New York the untrained Negroes not only form a very large class, but coming in contact, as they do, with foreigners who for generations have been forced to severe, unremitting toil, they suffer by comparison. The South in the days of slavery demanded chiefly routine work in the fields from its Negroes.[1] The work was under the direction either of the master, the overseer, or a foreman; and there has been no general advance in training for the colored men of the South since that time. Contrast the intensive cultivation of Italy or Switzerland with the farms of Georgia or Alabama, or the hotels of France with those of Virginia, and you will see the disadvantages from which the Negro suffers. America is young and crude, but opportunity has brought to her great cities workmen from all over the world. In New York these men are driven at a pace that at the outset distracts the colored man who prefers his leisurely way.

[1] See Ulrich B. Phillips' "Origin and Growth of the Southern Black Belts," *American Historical Review*, July, 1906.

Moreover, the foreign workmen have learned persistence; they are punctual and appear regularly each morning at their tasks. "The Italians are better laborers than any other people we have, are they not?" I asked a man familiar with many races and nationalities. "No," was his answer, "they do not work better than others, but when the whistle blows, they are always there." Mr. Stone, whose book I have already quoted a number of times, shows the irresponsible, fanciful wanderings of his Mississippi tenants, whom he endeavored, unsuccessfully, to establish in a permanent tenantry. The colored men in New York are far in advance of these farm hands, who are described as moving about simply because they desire a change, but they are also far from the steady, unswerving attitude of their foreign competitors. Inadequately educated, too often they come to New York with little equipment for tasks they must undertake successfully or starve — unless, puerile, they live by the labor of some industrious woman.

I have tried to depict the New York colored wage earners as they labor in the city today.

They are not a remarkable group, and were they white men, distinguished by some mark of nationality, they would pass without comment. But the Negro is on trial, and witnesses are continually called to tell of his failures and successes. We have seen that both in the attitude of the world about him, and in his own untutored self, there are many obstacles to prevent his advance; and his natural sensitiveness adds to these difficulties. He minds the coarse but often good-natured joke of his fellow laborer, and he remembers with a lasting pain the mortification of an employer's curt refusal of work. Had he the obtuseness of some Americans he would prosper better. As we have seen, many positions are completely closed to him, leading him to idleness and consequent crime. Just as not every able-bodied white man, who is out of work and impoverished, will go to the charities woodyard and saw wood, so not every colored man will accept the menial labor which may be the only work open to him. Instead, he may gamble or drift into a vagabond life. A well-known Philadelphia judge has said

that "The moral and intellectual advance
of a race is governed by the degree of its
industrial freedom. When that freedom is
restricted there is unbounded tendency to
drive the race discriminated against into the
ranks of the criminal." Discrimination in
New York has led many Negroes into these
ranks. But as we look back at the occupations of our colored men we see a large number who secure regular hours, and if a poor,
yet a fairly steady pay. For the mass of the
Negroes coming into the city these positions
are an advance over their former work.
Employment in a great mercantile establishment, though it be in the basement, carries
dignity with it, and educating demands of
punctuality, sobriety, and swiftness. Richard R. Wright, Jr., whose right to speak with
authority we have already noted, believes
that the "North has taught the Negro the
value of money; of economy; it has taught
more sustained effort in work, punctuality,
and regularity." It has also, I believe, in
its more regular hours of work, aided in the
upbuilding of the home.

I remember once waiting in the harbor of

Genoa while our ship was taking on a cargo. The captain walked the deck impatiently, and, as the Italians went in leisurely fashion about their task, declared, "If I had those men in New York I could get twice the amount of work out of them." That is what New York does; it works men hard and fast; sometimes it mars them; but it pays a better wage than Genoa, and there is an excitement and dash about it that attracts laborers from all parts of the earth. The black men come, insignificant in numbers, ready to do their part. They work and play and marry and bring up children, and as we watch them moving to and from their tasks the North seems to have brought to the majority of them something of liberty and happiness.

CHAPTER V

Earning a Living — Business and the Professions

If we walk west on Fifty-ninth Street, at Eighth Avenue, we come upon one of the colored business sections of New York. Here, for a block's length, are employment and real estate agents, restaurant keepers, grocers, tailors, barbers, printers, expressmen, and undertakers, all small establishments occupying the first floor or basement of some tenement or lodging house, and with the exception of the employment agency all patronized chiefly by the colored race. Another such section and a more prosperous one is in Harlem, on West One Hundred and Thirty-third, One Hundred and Thirty-fourth, and One Hundred and Thirty-fifth Streets. From the point of view of the whole business of the city such concerns are insignificant, but they are important from the

106

viewpoint of Negro progress, since they represent the accumulation of capital, experience in business methods, and hard work. Very slowly the New York Negro is meeting the demanding power of his people and is securing neighborhood trade that has formerly gone to the Italian and the Jew. Husband and wife, father and son, work in their little establishments and make a beginning in the mercantile world.

The Negro, as we have seen, has conducted businesses in New York in the past, businesses patronized chiefly by whites. Barbering and catering were his successes, and in both of these he has lost, despite the fact that one of the city's wealthiest colored men is a caterer. But if he has lost here, he has gained along other lines. Among a number of photographers he has one who is well-known for his excellent architectural work. Two manufacturers have brought out popular goods, the Haynes's razor strop, and the Howard shoe polish. These men, one a barber and one a Pullman car porter, improved upon implements used in their daily work and then turned to manufacture. The headquarters of the Howard shoe polish is in Chicago, where the firm employs thirty people, the New York branch giving employment to twelve.

A wise utilization of labor already trained and at hand is seen in the Manhattan House Cleaning and Renovating Bureau. This firm contracts for the cleaning of houses and places of business and has also been successful in securing work on new buildings, entering as the builders leave and arranging everything for occupancy. In one week the Bureau has given employment to sixty men.

In those businesses in which he comes in contact with the white, the most pronounced success of the colored man has been real estate brokerage. The New York Negro business directory names twenty-two real estate brokers, and though a dozen of them probably handle altogether no more business than one white firm, a few put through important operations. The ablest of these brokers, recently clearing twenty thousand dollars at a single transaction, turned his operations to Liberia, where he went for a few months to look into land concessions.

This broker has aided the Negroes materially in their efforts to rent apartments on better streets. His energy, and that of many more like him, is also needed to open up places for colored businesses, better office and workroom facilities for the able professional and business men and women. In New York as in the South the Negro needs to obtain a hold upon the land. In this he is aided not only by his brokers, but by realty companies. The largest of these, the Metropolitan Realty Company, in operation since 1900, is capitalized at a million dollars, and had in 1910 $400,000 paid in stock, and $400,000 subscribed and being paid for on instalment. This company operates in the suburban towns, and has quite a colony in Plainfield, New Jersey, where it owns 150 lots. It has built eighty cottages for its members, and has bought eighteen.

Among the businesses that cater directly to the colored, probably none is more successful than undertaking. The Negroes of the city die in great numbers, and the funeral is all too common a function. Formerly this business went to white men, but increasingly it is coming into the hands of the colored. The Negro business directory gives twenty-two undertakers, one of them, by common report, the richest colored man in New York. Profitable real estate investment, combined with one of the largest undertaking establishments in the city, has given him a comfortable fortune. Another large and increasingly important Negro business is the hotel and boarding-house. As the colored men of the South and West accumulate wealth, they will come in increasing numbers to visit in New York, and the colored hotel, now little more than a boarding-house, may become a spacious building, with private baths, elevator service, and a well-equipped restaurant. In today's modestly equipped buildings the catering is often excellent, and good, well-cooked food is sold at reasonable prices. Occasionally the Hotel Maceo advertises a southern dinner, and its guests sit down to Virginia sugar-cured ham, sweet potato pie, and perhaps even opossum.

Printing establishments, tailors' shops,[1]

[1] On West 133d Street two former Hampton students have a prosperous little tailor and upholstering shop.

express and van companies, and many other small enterprises help to make up the Negro business world. One colored printer brings out an important white magazine. There are seven weekly colored newspapers, of which the New York *Age* is the most important, and two musical publishing companies. All these enterprises are useful, not only to the proprietor and his patrons, but especially to the clerks and assistants who thus are able to secure some training in mercantile work. In the white man's office, white and colored boys start out together, but as their trousers lengthen and their ambitions quicken, the former secures promotion while the latter is still given the letters to put into the mail box. If the Negro lad, discouraged at lack of advancement, leaves the white man and ventures with a tiny capital into some business of his own, his ignorance is almost certain to lead to his disaster. He is indeed fortunate if he can first work in the office of a successful colored man.[1]

[1] Those interested in the Negro in business should look for an intensive study, shortly to be published, on the wage-earners and business enterprises among Negroes in New York. It is entitled "The Negro at Work in New York City," and

We have one more census division to consider, Professional Service. The table runs as follows:

PROFESSIONAL SERVICE

	Total number of males in each occupation.	Number of negroes in each occupation.	Number of Negroes to each 1000 workers in occupation.
Actors, professional showmen, etc.	4,733	254	54
Architects, designers, draftsmen ..	3,966	2	0
Artists, teachers of art	2,924	13	4
Clergymen	2,833	90	32
Dentists	1,509	25	16
Physicians and surgeons	6,577	32	5
Veterinary surgeons	320	2	6
Electricians	8,131	18	2
Engineers (civil) and surveyors ...	3,321	7	2
Journalists	2,833	7	2
Lawyers	7,811	26	3
Literary and scientific	1,709	10	5
Musicians....................	6,429	195	30
Officials (government)	3,934	9	2
Teachers and professors in colleges	3,409	32	9
Total including some occupations not specified	60,853	729	12

Examining these figures we find few colored architects[1] or engineers, and a very

has been made by George E. Haynes, under the direction of the Bureau of Social Research of the New York School of Philanthropy.

[1] Since going to press the new and very beautiful building

small proportion of electricians, though among the latter there is a highly skilled workman. The New York Negro has no position in the mechanical arts. It may be that, as we so often hear, the African does not possess mechanical ability.[1] You do not see Negro boys pottering over machinery or making toy inventions of their own. But another and powerful reason for the colored youth's failing to take up engineering or kindred studies is the slight chance he would later have in securing work. No group of men in America have opposed his progress more persistently than skilled mechanics, and, should he graduate from some school of technology, he would be refused in office or workshop. So he

of St. Philips' Episcopal Church, on W. 134th Street, has been opened. This is a fine example of English Gothic and its architects are two young colored men, one of whom was for years in the office of a white firm.

[1] Mary Kingsley has some interesting generalizations on this point. She speaks of the African mind approaching all things from a spiritual point of view while the English mind approaches them from a material point of view, and of "the high perception of justice you will find in the African, combined with the inability to think out a pulley or a lever except under white tuition." — *West African Studies*, p. 330.

turns to those professions in which he sees a likelihood of advancement.

Colored physicians and dentists are increasing in number in New York and throughout the country. The Negro is sympathetic, quick to understand another's feelings, and when added to this he has received a thorough medical training he makes an excellent physician. New York State examinations prevent the practice of ignorant doctors from other states, and the city can count many able colored practitioners. These doctors practise among white people as well as among colored. As surgeons they are handicapped in New York by lack of hospital facilities, having no suitable place in which they may perform an operation. The colored student who graduates from a New York medical college must go for hospital training to Philadelphia or Chicago or Washington.[1]

---

[1] Lincoln Hospital in New York, while receiving white and colored patients, was especially designed to help the colored race. It has a training school for colored nurses, but neither accepts colored medical graduates as interns, nor allows colored doctors upon its staff. This is one of many cases in which the good white people of the city are glad to assist the poor and ailing Negro, but are unwilling to help the strong and ambitious colored man to full opportunity.

Colored lawyers are obtaining a firm foot-hold in New York. From twenty-six in the 1900 census they now, in 1911, number over fifty, though not all of these by any means rely entirely upon their profession for support. Some of our lawyers are descendants of old New York families, others have come here recently from the South.

Turning to our census figures again we see that the three professions in which the colored man is conspicuous are those of actor, musician, and minister. Instead of the average eighteen, he here shows fifty-four in every thousand actors, thirty in every thousand musicians, and thirty-two in every thousand clergymen. And since the pulpit and the stage are two places in which the black man has found conspicu-ous success it may be well in this connec-tion to consider, not only the economic significance of these institutions, but their place in the life of the colored world.

The Negro minister was born with the Negro Christian, and the colored church, in which he might tell of salvation, is over

a century old in New York. Today the
Boroughs of Manhattan and Brooklyn have
twenty-eight colored churches besides a
number of missions. Some of the societies
own valuable property, usually, however,
encumbered with heavy mortgages, and
yearly budgets mount up to ten, twelve,
and sixteen thousand dollars. The Methodist churches lead in number, next come
the Baptist, and next the Episcopalian.
There are Methodist Episcopal, African
Methodist Episcopal, and African Methodist Episcopal Zion. Bethel African Methodist Episcopal Church, as we have seen, is
one of the oldest and is still one of the
largest and most useful Negro churches in
New York. Mount Olivet, a Baptist church
on West Fifty-third Street, has a seating
capacity of 1600, taxed to its full on Sunday evenings. St. Philip's gives the Episcopal service with dignity and devoutness,
and its choir has many sweet colored boy
singers. At St. Benedict, the Moor, the
black faces of the boy acolytes contrast
with the benignant white-haired Irish priest,
and without need of words preach good-

will to men. Only in this Catholic church
does one find white and black in almost
equal numbers worshipping side by side.

The great majority of the colored churches
are supported by their congregations, and
the minister or elder, or both, twice a Sunday, must call for the pennies and nickels,
dimes and quarters, that are dropped into
the plate at the pulpit's base. Contribu-
tors file past the table on which they place
their offering, emulation becoming a spur
to generosity. These collections are supplemented by sums raised at entertainments
and fairs, and it is in this way, by the
constant securing of small gifts, that the
thousands are raised.

The church is a busy place and retains
its members, not only by its preaching, but
by midweek meetings. There are the class
meetings of the Methodists, the young people's societies, the prayer meetings, and
the sermons preached to the secret benefit
organizations. Visiting sisters and brothers
attend to relief work, and standing at a
side table, sometimes picturesque with lighted
lantern, ask for dole for the poor.

The Sunday-schools, while not so large as the church attendance would lead one to expect, involve much time and labor in their conduct. A colored church member finds all his or her leisure occupied in church work. I know a young woman engaged in an exacting, skilled profession who spends her day of rest attending morning service, teaching in Sunday-school, taking part in the young people's lyceum in the late afternoon, and listening to a second sermon in the evening. Occasionally she omits her dinner to hear an address at the colored Young Men's Christian Association. On hot summer afternoons you may see colored boys and girls and men and women crowded in an ill-ventilated hall, giving ear to a fervid exhortation that leads the speaker, at the sentence's end, to mop his swarthy face. The woods, the salt-smelling sea, the tamer prettiness of the lawns of the city's park, have not the impelling call of sermon or hymn. If the whole of the Negro's summer Sunday is to be given to direct religious teaching, one wishes that it might take place at the old time camp meeting, where there is fresh air and space in which to breathe it. The first of Edward Everett Hale's three rules of life as he gave them to the Hampton students was, "Live all you can out in the open air." The religious-minded New York Negro succumbs easily to disease, and yet elects to spend his day of leisure within doors.

With the exception of the Episcopalians, the churches undertake little institutional work. Money is lacking, and there is only a feeble conviction of the value of the gymnasium, pool table, and girls' and boys' clubs. The colored branches of the Young Men's Christian Association, however, are places for recreation and instruction. The lines that Evangelical Americans draw regarding amusements, prohibiting cards and welcoming dominos, allowing bagatelle and frowning upon billiards, must be interpreted by some folk-lore historian to show their reasonableness. Doubtless the extent to which a game is used for gambling purposes has much to do with its good or bad savor, and pool and cards for this reason are tabooed. Dancing is also frowned upon

by many of the churches, while temperance
societies make active campaign for prohi-
bition. To New York's black folk, the
church-goers and they who stand without
are the sheep and the goats, and the gulf
between them is digged deep.

Of the five colored Episcopal churches, St.
Philip's and St. Cyprian's have parish houses.
St. Philip's has moved into a new parish
house on West One Hundred and Thirty-
Fourth Street, where with its large, well-
arranged rooms, its gymnasium, and its corps
of enthusiastic workers it will soon become
a powerful force in the Harlem Negro's life.
St. Cyprian's is under the City Episcopal
Mission, and has unusual opportunity for
helpfulness since it is separated only by
Amsterdam Avenue from the San Juan Hill
district and yet stands amid the whites.
Its clubs and classes, its employment agency,
its gymnasium, its luncheons for school
children, its beautiful church, are all prima-
rily for the Negroes; but the colored rector
has a friendly word for his white neighbors,
tow-headed Irish and German boys and girls
sit upon his steps, and his ministry has

lessened the belligerent feeling between the east and the west sides of Amsterdam Avenue. St. David's Episcopal Church in the Bronx has a fresh air home at White Plains, cared for personally by the rector and his wife, who spend their vacation with tenement mothers and their children, the tired but grateful recipients of their good-will.

If there were ninety colored clergymen in New York in 1900, as the census says, a number must have been without churches, itinerant preachers or directors of small missions, supporting themselves by other labor during the day. Those men who now fill the pulpits of well-established churches have been trained in theological schools of good standing, for the ignorant "darky" of the story who leaves the hot work of the cotton field because he feels a "call" to preach does not receive another from New York. The colored minister in this city works hard and long, and finds a wearying number of demands upon his time. The wedding and the funeral, the word of counsel to the young, and of comfort to the aged,

a multiplicity of meetings, two sermons
every Sunday, the continual strain of raising money, these are some of his duties.
With a day from fourteen to seventeen hours
long he earns as few men earn the meagre
salary put into his hand. But his position
among his people is a commanding one, and
carries with it respect and responsibility.

Strangers who visit colored churches to
be amused by the vociferations of the
preacher and the responses of the congregation will be disappointed in New York.
Others, however, who attend, desiring to
understand the religious teaching of the
thoughtful Negro, find much of interest.
They hear sermons marked by great elo-
quence. In the Evangelical church the
preacher is not afraid to give his imagination play, and in finely chosen, vivid language, pictures his thought to his people.
Especially does he love to tell the story of
a future life, of Paradise with its rapturous
beauty of color and sound, its golden streets,
its gates of precious stones, effulgent, radi-
ant. He dwells not upon the harshness,
but rather upon the mercy of God.

A theological library connected with a Calvinistic church, when recently catalogued, disclosed two long shelves of books upon Hell and two slim volumes upon Heaven. No such unloving Puritanism dominates the Negro's thought. Hell's horrors may be portrayed at a revival to bring the sinner to repentance, but only as an aid to a clearer vision of the glories of Heaven.

The Negro churches lay greater stress than formerly upon practical religion; they try to turn a fine frenzy into a determination for righteousness. This was strikingly exemplified lately in one of New York's colored Baptist churches. During the solemn rite of immersion the congregation began to grow hysterical, or "happy," as they would have phrased it; there were cries of "Yes, Jesus," "We're comin', Lord," and swayings of the body backward and forward. The minister with loud and stirring appeal for a time encouraged these emotions. Then in a moment he brought quiet to his congregation and called them to the consecration of labor. Faith without works was vain. Baptism was not the end, but only the begin-

ning of their salvation. "You-all bleege
ter work," he said, "if yer gwine foller der
Lord. Ain't Jesus work in der carpenter
shop till he nigh on thirty year old? Den
one day he stood up (he ain't none er yer
two-by-fo' men) an' he tak off his blue apun
(I reckon he wore er apun like we-alls) an'
he goes on down ter der wilderness, an'
John der Baptist baptize him."

From oratory one turns naturally to
music. The feeling for rhythm, for melodi-
ous sound, that leads the Negro to use
majestic words of which he has not always
mastered the meaning, leads him also to
musical expression. He has an instinct
for harmony, and, when within hearing dis-
tance of any instrument, will whistle, not
the melody, however assertive, but will
add a part.[1] Those who have visited colored schools, and especially the colored
schools of the far South where the pupils
are unfamiliar with other music than their
own, can never forget the exquisite, haunt-
ing singing. When a foreman wants to get

[1] See H. J. Wilson, "The Negro and Music," *Outlook*,
Dec. 1, 1906.

energetic work from his black laborers he sets them to singing stirring tunes. The Negro has his labor songs as the sailor has his chanties, and it would be impossible to measure the joy coming to both through musical expression.

In New York, despite their poverty, few Negroes fail to possess some musical instrument — a banjo perhaps, or a guitar, a mandolin or zither, or it may be the highly prized piano. Visiting of an evening in the Phipps model tenement, one hears a variety of gay tinkling sounds. And besides the mechanical instruments there is always the great natural instrument, the human voice. Singing, though not as common in the city as in the country, is still often heard, especially in the summer, and remains musical, though New York's noise and cheap and vulgar entertainments have an unhappy fashion of roughening her children's voices.

Music furnishes a means of livelihood to many Negroes and supplements the income of many others. Boys contribute to the family support by singing cheap songs in saloons or even in houses of prostitution.

A boy "nightingale" will earn the needed money for rent while learning, all too quickly, the ways of viciousness. Others, more carefully reared, sing at church or secret society concert, perhaps receiving a little pay. Men form male quartettes that for five or ten dollars furnish a part of an evening's entertainment. There are many Negro musicians and elocutionists who largely support themselves by their share in the receipts from concerts and social gatherings.

We speak of men crossing the line when they intermarry with the whites, but there is another crossing of the line when some Negro by his genius makes the world forget his race. Such a man is the artist, Henry Tanner; and New York has such Negro musicians. Mr. Harry Burleigh, the baritone at St. George's, has won high recognition, not only as an interpreter, but as a composer of music; and one of the richest synagogues of the city has a Negro for its assistant organist. There are five colored orchestras in New York, the one conducted by Mr. Walter A. Craig having toured

successfully in New England and many other
northern states.

But the colored musician has usually
found his opportunity for expression and
for a living wage upon the stage. Probably
many of the actors noted on the census list
are musicians, and many of the musicians,
actors; the writer of the topical song having
himself sung it in vaudeville or musical
comedy. Few New Yorkers appreciate how
many of the tunes hummed in the street
or ground out on the hand-organ, have orig-
inated in Negro brains. "The Right Church
but the Wrong Pew," "Teasing," "Nobody,"
"Under the Bamboo Tree," which Cole and
Johnson, the composers, heard the last
thing as they left the dock in New York, and
the first thing when they arrived in Paris,
these are a few of the popular favorites.
Handsome incomes have been netted by the
shrewder among these composers, and the
demand for their songs is continuous.

With a bright song and a jolly dance
comes success. Picking up the copy of the
New York *Age*, that lies on my desk, I find
jottings of twenty-four colored troupes in

vaudeville in the larger cities of the North
and West. Three are at Proctor's and three
at Keith's. Their economic outlook is not
so hilarious as their songs, for transporta-
tion is expensive and bookings are uncertain; yet pecuniarily these actors are far
better off than their more sober brothers
who stick to their elevators or their porters'
jobs.

Twenty years ago the Negro performer
probably had little anticipation of advancing
beyond minstrel work, in which he sang
loud, danced hard, and told a funny story.
S. H. Dudley, the leading comedian in the
"Smart Set" colored company, said in
1909: "When I started in business I had
no idea of getting as high as I am now. A
minstrel company came to the little town in
Texas where I was raised, and at once my
ambition fired me to become a musician.
So I bought a battered horn and began to
toot, to the great annoyance of my neighbors.
Then I secured an engagement with a minstrel company whose cornet player had
fallen into the hands of the law; and now
here I am with one of the best colored shows

ever gotten together and a starring tour arranged for next season." The movement from the minstrel show to the musical comedy, from the cheapest form of buffoonery to attractive farce, and even to good comedy, has been accomplished by a number of colored comedians. Williams and Walker may be considered the pioneers in this movement, and the story of their success, as Walker has told it, is a fine example of what the Negro can do along the line of decided natural aptitude. And it is important to notice this, for today, in the education of the race, æsthetic instincts are often suppressed with Puritan vigor, and labor is made ugly and unwelcome.

Bert Williams and George Walker, one a British West Indian, the other a Westerner, met in California where each was hanging around a box manager's office, looking for a job. Hardly more than boys, they secured employment at seven dollars a week. That was in 1889. In 1908 they made each $250 a week, and in later times they have doubled and quadrupled this. Their first stage manager expected them to perform as

the blacked-up white minstrels were performing, but the two boys soon saw that the
Negro himself was far more entertaining than
the buffoon portrayed by the white man.
They wanted to show the true Negro, and
billing themselves as the "real coons" (their
white rivals called themselves "coons") they
played in San Francisco with some success.
Later they came to New York, and at Koster
and Bial's made their first hit.

"Long before our run terminated," Walker
said in telling of those early days, "we dis-
covered an important fact: that the hope of
the colored performer must be in making a
radical departure from the old time 'darky'
style of singing and dancing. So we set
ourselves the task of thinking along new
lines.

"The first move was to hire a flat in
Fifty-third Street, furnish it, and throw our
doors open to all colored men who possessed
theatrical and musical ability and ambition. The Williams and Walker flat soon
became the headquarters of all the artistic
young men of our race who were stage-
struck. We entertained the late Paul Law-

rence Dunbar, who wrote lyrics for us.
By having these men about us we had the
opportunity to study the musical and theatrical ability of the most talented members
of our race."

In 1893 the World's Fair was held at
Chicago, and on the "Midway" the visitor
saw races from all over the world. Here
was a Dahomey village, with strange little
huts, representative of the African home
life. The Dahomeyans themselves were late
in arriving, and American Negroes, sometimes with an added coat of black, were
employed to represent them. Among them
were Williams and Walker, who played
their parts until the real Dahomeyans arriving, they became in turn spectators and
studied the true African. This contact
with the dancing and singing of the primi-
tive people of their own race had an important effect upon their art. Their lyrics
recalled African songs, their dancing took
on African movements, especially Walker's.
Any one who saw Walker in "Abyssinia,"
the most African and the most artistic of
their plays, must have recognized the

savage beauty of his dancing when he was masquerading as an African king.

After the Dahomey episode the success of the two men was continuous. "In 1902 and 1903," Walker said, "we had all New York and London doing the cake walk." In February, 1908, they appeared in "Bandanna Land," at the Majestic Theatre, and remained there for six months. Only those colored men who have made a steady, uphill struggle for the chance to play good comedy, know how important such recognition was for the Negro. "Bandanna Land" was probably the most popular light opera in New York that winter next to "The Merry Widow." The singing, especially that of the male chorus, was often beautiful. Mrs. Walker's dancing and charming acting were delightful, the chorus girls were above the average in beauty and musical expression, and the two men who made the piece were spontaneously, irresistibly funny; added to this, unlike its successful rival, "Bandanna Land" was without a vulgar scene or word.

This was the last time the two men played

together. Walker became seriously ill, and
died in January, 1911. After their company
disbanded, Williams went back to the one-
piece act of vaudeville, but as a star in a
white troupe. His position as a permanent
actor in the "Follies of 1910" marks a new
departure for the colored comedian, a departure won by great talent combined with
character and tact.

Since 1908 the Majestic has seen another
colored company, Cole and Johnson's, pre-
senting a half-Negro, half-Indian, musical
comedy, the "Red Moon." These two men,
for years in vaudeville, have written songs
for Lillian Russell, Marie Cahill, Anna Held,
and other popular musical comedy and
vaudeville singers. They have played for six
months continuously at the Palace Theatre,
London. Accustomed to writing for white
actors, their own plays are not so distinct-
ively African as Williams and Walker's.
Both Johnson and Cole are of the mulatto
type, and neither blackens his face. Cole
is one of the most amusing men in comedy
in New York. He is tall and very thin,
with a genius for finding lank and gro-

tesque costumes that are delightfully incon-
gruous with his grave face. The words of
the musical comedies are his, the music,
Johnson's. He, too, has become seriously
ill, and his company has disbanded. In
three years the colored stage has suffered
serious loss, but we see forming new and
successful companies whose reputation will
soon be assured.

Comedy has always furnished a medium
for criticism of the foibles of the times, and
there are many sly digs at the white man
in the colored play. Ernest Hogan, now
deceased, better than any one else played
the rural southern darky. In the "Oyster-
man" we saw him in contact with a white
scamp who was intent upon getting his recently acquired money. He was urged to
take stock in a land company, to buy where
watermelons grew as thick as potatoes,
and chickens were as common as sparrows.
The audience hated the white man heartily
and sided with the simple, kindly, black
youth, sitting with his dog at his side, on
his cabin steps. Behind boisterous laughter
and raillery the writers of these comedies

often gain the sympathy of their hearers
for the black race.

In this attempt to show the occupational
life of the Negro, we have found that race
prejudice often proves a bar to complete
success, to full manhood. Something of this
is true with the actor as well as with the
laborer and the business man. In securing
entrance in vaudeville, color is at first an
advantage. The "darky" to the white man
is grotesquely amusing, and by rolling his
eyes, showing a glistening smile, and wearing shoes that make a monstrosity of his
feet, the Negro may create a laugh where
the man with a white skin would be hooted
off the stage. And since the laugh is so
easily won, many colored actors become
indolent and content themselves, year after
year, with playing the part of buffoon.
But with the ambition to rise in his profession comes the difficult struggle to induce
the audience to see a new Negro in the black
man of today. The public gives the colored man no opportunity as a tragedian,
demanding that his comedy shall border
always on the farcical. And what is de-

manded of the actor is also demanded of the
musician. Writers of the scores of some
of our musical comedies are musicians of
superior training and ability, but rarely
are they permitted full expression. Mr.
Will Marion Cook, the composer of much of
the music of "Bandanna Land," for a few
moments gives a piece of exquisite orches-
tration. When the colored minister rises
and exhorts his quarrelling friends to be at
peace with one another, one hears a beautiful harmony. I am told that Mr. Cook
declares that the next score he writes shall
begin with ten minutes of serious music.
If the audience doesn't like it, they can come
in late, but for ten minutes he will do something worthy of his genius.

However light-hearted a people, and however worthy of praise the entertainment
that brings a jolly, wholesome laugh, let
us hope that in the near future the Negro
will find a more complete expression for
his musical and histrionic gifts. Some actor
of commanding talent, whose claims cannot
be ignored, may reveal the larger life of
the race. The nineteenth century knew a

great Negro actor, Ira Aldridge, a *protégé* and disciple of Edmund Kean. He played Othello to Kean's Iago, and in the forties toured Europe with his own company, receiving high honors in Berlin and St. Petersburg.[1] A dark-skinned African, of immense power, physically and emotionally, he made Desdemona cry out in real fear, and caused Bassanio instinctively to shrink as he demanded his pound of flesh. Today's actor must be more subtle in his attack, but it may be given to him to reveal the thoughts at the back of the black man's mind. The genius of Zangwill gave us the picture of the children of the Ghetto; perhaps from the theatre's seat the American will first understand the despised black race.

[1] William J. Simmons's, "Men of Mark."

CHAPTER VI

The Colored Woman as a Bread Winner

The life of the Negro woman of New York, if she belong to the laboring class, differs in some important respects from the life of the white laboring woman. Generalizations on so comprehensive a subject must, of course, meet with many exceptions, but the observing visitor, familiar with white and colored neighborhoods, quickly notes marked contrasts between the two, contrasts largely the result of different occupational opportunities. These pertain both to the married woman and the unmarried working girl.

The generality of white women in New York, wives of laboring men, infrequently engage in gainful occupations. In the early years of married life the wife relies on her husband's wage for support, and within her tiny tenement-flat bears and rears her chil-

dren and performs her household duties —
the sewing, cooking, washing, and ironing,
and the daily righting of the contracted
rooms. She is a conscientious wife and
mother, and rarely, either by night or by day,
journeys far from her own home. When unemployment visits the family wage earner,
she turns to laundry work and day's cleaning
for money to meet the rent and to supply the
household with scanty meals; but as soon as
her husband resumes work she returns to
her narrow round of domestic duties.

After a score of these monotonous years
more prosperous times come to the housewife. Every morning two or three children
go out to work, and their wages make heavier
the family purse. Son and daughter, having
entered factory or store, bring home their
pay envelopes unbroken on Saturday nights,
and the augmentation of the father's wage
gives the mother an income to administer.
After the young people's wants in clothing
and entertainment have been in part sup-
plied, it becomes possible to buy new furniture on the instalment plan, to hire a piano,
even to move into a better neighborhood.

The earnings of a number of children, supplementing the wage of the head of the family, make life more tolerable for all.

These days, however, do not last long. Sons and daughters marry and assume new responsibilities; the husband, his best strength gone, finds unemployment increasing; and since saving, except for wasteful industrial insurance, has seemed impossible without sacrificing the decencies and pleasures of the children, the end of the woman's married life is likely to be hard and comfortless.

This rough description may fairly be taken to represent the life of the average New York white woman of the laboring class. It is not, however, the life of the average colored woman. With her, self-sustaining work usually begins at fifteen, and by no means ceases with her entrance upon marriage, which only entails new financial burdens. The wage of the husband, as we have seen, is usually insufficient to support a family, save in extreme penury, and the wife accepts the necessity of supplementing the husband's income. This she accomplishes by taking in washing or by entering a private family to do housework. Sometimes she is away from her tenement nearly every day in the week; again the bulk of her earnings comes from home industry. Her day holds more diversity than that of her white neighbor; she meets more people, becomes familiar with the ways of the well-to-do, — their household decorations, their dress, their refinements of manner; but she has but few hours to give to her children. With her husband she is ready to be friend and helpmate; but should he turn out a bad bargain, she has no fear of leaving him, since her marital relations are not welded by economic dependence. An industrious, competent woman, she works and spends, and in her scant hours of leisure takes pride in keeping her children well-dressed and clean.

At the second period of her married life, when her boys and girls, few in number if she be a New Yorker, begin to engage in self-supporting work, her condition shows less improvement than that of the white woman of her class. Sometimes her children hand her their whole wage, far oftener they bring her only such part as they choose

to spare. The strict accounting of the minor
to the parent, usual among Northerners in
the past, and today common among the
immigrant class, is not a part of the Negro's
training. Rather, as the race has attained
freedom it has copied the indulgent attitude
of the once familiar "master," and regrets
that its offspring must enter upon any work.
Children with this tradition about them use
the money they earn largely for the gratifica-
tion of their vanity, not for the lessening of
their mother's tasks. But a more potent
factor than lack of discipline keeps the
mother from being the administrator of the
family's joint earnings. White boys and
girls in New York enter work that makes it
possible and advantageous for them to dwell
at home; Negroes must go out to service,
accept long and irregular hours in hotel or
apartment, travel for days on boat or train.
The family home is infrequently available
to them, and money given in to it brings
small return. Under these circumstances it
is not strange if the mother must continue
her round of washing and scrubbing.

The last years of life of the Negro woman,

probably a little more than the last years of
the white, are likely to bring happiness.
With a mother at work a grandmother
becomes an important factor, and elderly
colored women are often seen bringing up
little children or helping in the laundry —
that great colored home industry. Accustomed all their lives to hard labor, it is easy
for them to find work that shall repay their
support, and in their children's households
they are treated with respect and consideration.

The contrast in the lives of the colored and
white married women is not more strongly
marked than the contrast in the lives of their
unmarried daughters and sisters. Unable to
enter any pursuit except housework, the
unskilled colored girl goes out to service or
helps at home with the laundry or sewing.
Factory and store are closed to her, and
rarely can she take a place among other
working girls. Her hours are the long, irregular hours of domestic service. She brings
no pay envelope home to her mother, the
two then carefully discussing how much
belongs rightfully for board, and how much

may go for the new coat or dress, but takes the eighteen or twenty dollars given her at the end of the month, and quite by herself determines all her expenditures. Far oftener than any class of white girls in the city she lives away from the parental home.

These are some of the differences found by the observer who looks into the Negro and the white tenement. They need not, however, rest alone upon any observer's testimony. We have in the census abundant statistics for their verification. Scattered among the volumes on Population, Occupations, and Women at Work are many facts concerning Negro women workers of New York, all of them confirmatory of the description just given. We may note the most important.

In 1900, whereas 4.2 per cent of the white married women in New York were engaged in gainful occupations, 31.4 per cent of the Negro married women were earning their living, over seven times as many in proportion as the whites.[1]

[1] These figures are obtained by a combination of tables, one in Population, Vol. II, Part II, p. 332, describing the whole

Again, in the total population of New York's women workers, 80 per cent were single, 10 per cent married, and 10 per cent widowed and divorced; while among the Negroes, the single women were only 53 per cent, the married 25 per cent, and the widowed 22.[1]

Statistics of the age period at which women are at work, show the Negro's long continuing wage-earning activity. Between sixteen and twenty is a busy time for the women of both races. Among the whites 59 per cent are in gainful occupations, among the Negroes 66 per cent. But as the girl arrives at the period when she is likely to marry, the per cent of workers among the whites drops rapidly, until for white women, forty-five and over, it is 13.5, about one in seven. With the colored, among the women forty-five years of age and over, 53

of Greater New York, the other in Women at Work, pp. 266 to 275, describing Manhattan, the Bronx, and Brooklyn. The error through the omission of Richmond and Queens is probably negligible.

[1] Federal Census 1900: Women at Work, Table 28, pp. 266 to 274. Among 800 married and widowed colored women whom I myself visited, I found only 150, 19 per cent, who were not engaged in gainful occupations.

per cent, more than half, still engage in gainful toil.[1]

Family life can be studied in the census table. While 59 per cent of the unmarried white girls at work live at home, this is found to be true of but 25 per cent of the colored girls; that is, 75 per cent, three-quarters of all the colored unmarried working women, live with their employers or board.[2]

The census volume on occupations reveals at once the narrow range of the New York colored woman's working life. Personal and domestic service absorbs 90 per cent of her numbers against 40 per cent among the white. But before considering more fully the colored girl at work, we need to notice another statistical fact, the preponderance in the city of Negro women over Negro men.

Like the foreigner, the youth of the Negro race comes first to the city to seek a livelihood. The colored population shows 41 per cent of its number between the ages of 20

[1] Federal Census 1900: Women at Work, Table 10, pp. 147 to 151.

[2] Federal Census 1900: Women at Work, Table 28, pp. 266 to 275.

and 35.   But unlike the foreigner, the Negro women find larger opportunity and come in greater numbers than the men.   Their range of work is narrow, but within it they can command double the wages they receive at home, and if they are possessed of average ability, they are seldom long out of work. With the immense growth of wealth in New York the demand for servants continually increases, and finding little response from the white native born population, many mistresses receive readily the services of the English-speaking southern and West Indian blacks.   So the boats from Charleston and Norfolk and the British West Indies bring scores and hundreds of Negro women from country districts, from cities where they have spent a short time at service, girls with and girls without experience, all seeking better wages in a new land.

Mr. Kelly Miller was the first to call attention to the presence in American cities of surplus Negro women.[1]   The phenomenon is not peculiar to New York.   Baltimore,

[1] This is incorporated in a chapter in Mr. Miller's volume on "Race Adjustment."

Washington, New Orleans, all show the same condition. In Atlanta the women number 143 to every hundred colored men. New York shows 123 to every masculine one hundred. These surplus women account in part for the number of Negro women workers in New York not living at home. Some are with their employers, but others lodge in the already crowded tenements, for the southern servant, unaccustomed to spending the night at her employer's, in New York also, frequently arranges to leave her mistress when her work is done. In their hours of leisure the surplus women are known to play havoc with their neighbors' sons, even with their neighbors' husbands, for since lack of men makes marriage impossible for about a fifth of New York's colored girls, social disorder results. Surplus Negro women, able to secure work, support idle, able-bodied Negro men. The lounger at the street corner, the dandy in the parlor thrumming on his banjo, means a Malindy of the hour at the kitchen washboard. In a town in Germany, where men were sadly scarce, I was told that a servant girl paid as high as a mark to a soldier to walk with her in the Hofgarten on a Sunday afternoon. Colored men in New York command their "mark," and girls are found who keep them in polished boots, fashionable coats, and well-creased trousers. Could the Negro country boy be as certain as his sister of lucrative employment in New York, or could he oftener persuade her to remain with him on the farm, he would better city civilization. But the demand for servants increases, and the colored girl continues to be attracted to the city where she can earn and spend.

The table on the following page shows in condensed form the occupations of the Negro women in New York. As we see, the Negro women number forty-four in every thousand women workers.

Ninety per cent of all the Negro women workers of New York are in domestic and personal service. This includes a variety of positions. Some Negro girls work in stores, dusting stock, taking charge of cloak or toilet rooms, scrubbing floors. Their hours are regular, but the pay, five or six, or very occasionally eight dollars a week, means a

scanty livelihood without hope of advancement. The position of maid in a theatre
where perquisites are larger is prized, and a
new and pleasant place is that of a maid on

FEMALES TEN YEARS OF AGE AND OVER, ENGAGED IN
GAINFUL OCCUPATIONS IN NEW YORK

	Total	Negro	Number to every 1000 workers
Professional service	22,422	281	12
Domestic and personal service	146,722	14,586	100
Laundresses	16,102	3,224	200
Servants and waitresses	103,963	10,297	99
All others	24,657	1,065	43
Trade and transportation	65,318	106	Between one and two
Manufacturing and mechanical pursuits ...	132,535	1,138	7
Dressmakers	37,514	813	22
Seamstresses	18,108	249	14
All others	76,913	76	1
Total including some occupations not specified ..	367,437	16,114	44

Federal Census 1900: Occupations, Table 43, p. 638

a limited train. But the bulk of the girls
are servants in boarding-houses, or are with
private families as nurses, waitresses, cooks,
laundresses, maids-of-all-work, earning from

sixteen and eighteen to twenty-five and even thirty dollars a month. Occasionally a very skilful cook can command as high a monthly wage as fifty dollars.

The colored girl is frequently found engaged at general housework in a small apartment. Her desire to return to her lodging at night makes her popular with families living in contracted space. With the conveniences of a New York flat, dumb-waiter, clothes-dryer, gas, and electricity, general housework is not severe. Work begins early, seven at the latest, and lasts until the dinner is cleared away, at half-past eight or nine. Released then from further tasks, the young girl goes to her tiny inner tenement room, dons a fresh dress, and then, as chance or her training determines, walks the streets, goes to the theatre, or attends the class meeting at her church. Entertainments among the Negroes are rarely under way until ten o'clock, and short hours of sleep in ill-ventilated rooms soon weaken the vitality of the new-comer. Housework under these conditions does not create much ambition; the mistress moves, flitting, in New York fashion, from one flat to another, and the girl also flits among employers, changing with the whim of the moment.

Few subjects present so fascinating a field for discussion as domestic service, and the housewife of today enters into it with energy, sometimes decrying the modern working girl, again planning household economics that shall lure her from factory or shop. The only point we need to consider now is the dissatisfaction that results when 64 per cent of the women of a race are forced by circumstances into one occupation. Those with native ability along this line succeed and make others and themselves happy. The faithful, patient, loyal Negro servant is well-known, the black mammy has passed into American literature, but not every colored woman can wisely be given this position. Some of the Negro girls who take up housework in New York are capable of more intelligent labor, and chafe under their limitations; others have not the ability to do good housework; for domestic service requires more mental capacity than is demanded in many factories. In short, a great many colored girls in

New York are round pegs in square holes, and the community is the loser by it.

Among these round pegs are girls who, determining no longer to drudge in lonely kitchens, contrive, as we shall see later, to find positions at other more attractive reputable work. Others, deciding in favor of material betterment at whatever cost, lower their moral standard and secure easier and more remunerative jobs. A well-paying place, with short hours and high tips, at once offers itself to the colored girl who is willing to work for a woman of the demi-monde. In the sporting house also she is preferred as a servant, her dark complexion separating her from other inmates. In 1858, Sanger wrote in his "History of Prostitution," "The servants (in these houses) are almost always colored women. Their wages are liberal, their perquisites considerable, and their work light." Untrained herself, bereft of home influence, with an ancestry that sometimes cries out her parent's weakness in the contour and color of her face, the Negro girl in New York, more even than the foreign immigrant, is subject to degrading temptation. The good people, who are often so exacting, want her for her willingness to work long hours at a lower wage than the white; and the bad people, who are often so carelessly kind, offer her light labor and generous pay. It is small wonder that she sometimes chooses the latter.

Not all the colored girls who work in questionable places and with questionable people take the jobs from choice; some are sent without knowing the character of the house they enter. A few years ago an agitation was started for the protection of helpless Negro immigrants who had fallen into the hands of unscrupulous employment agencies. A system existed, and still exists, by which employment agencies were able to advance the travelling expenses of southern girls, who on their arrival in New York were held in debt until the cost of the journey had been many times repaid. Helpless in the power of the agent, the new-comer was forced to work where he wished. Under the city's department of licenses some of the more unscrupulous of these agencies have been closed, and philanthropy has placed a visitor at the docks to give aid and advice to unprotected girls. But the danger is by no means over. Those familiar with the subject assert that there is a proportionately larger black slave than white slave traffic.

There is a gainful occupation for women, black and white, too important to be left unnoticed. The census does not tabulate it. The best people strive to ignore it, and carefully sheltered girls grow up unconscious of its existence. But the employment agent understands its commercial value, and little children in the red light neighborhood are as familiar with it as with the vending of peanuts on the street. To the poor it is always an open door affording at least a temporary respite from dispossession and starvation. How many of the colored turn to it, we do not know — certainly not a few. Some gain from it a meagre livelihood, but others, for a time at least, achieve comfort and even luxury.

Among the round pegs that the square holes so uncomfortably chafe are colored girls of intelligence and charm who deliberately join the anti-social class. Probably a few in any case would lead this life, but the history of many shows an unsuccessful struggle for congenial work, ending with a choice of material comfort however high the moral cost. In One Hundred and Thirty-fourth and One Hundred and Thirty-fifth Streets are apartments where such girls live, two or three together, surrounded by comforts that their respectable neighbors who go out to cook, wash, and iron may fruitlessly long for all their lives. A colored philanthropic worker, stopping by chance at the door of one of these places, saw an old college friend. "How can you do it!" she cried as she recognized the life the girl was leading, "How can you do it! I would rather kill myself scrubbing!" "There is the difference between us," came the answer, "I am not willing to die, and I cannot and will not scrub."

It is pleasant and encouraging to turn from colored women who have given up the struggle, to ambitious, successful workers. Some among these are in the domestic service group and enjoy with heartiness their tasks as nurse-maid or cook. "This is my piano day," an expert colored washerwoman says of a Monday morning. Among the domestic service workers, as classified by the census, is the trained nurse, filling an increasingly important position in New York. In 1909, Lincoln Hospital graduated twenty-one colored nurses, some of whom remain in New York to do excellent work.

In the professions, with the women as with the men, the first place numerically is occupied by performers upon the stage. So much has been said of the Negro as an actor that there is little to add. A rather better class of colored than of white women join musical comedy chorus troupes, for fifteen or eighteen dollars a week that will attract a Negro to the stage can be made by a white girl in a dozen other ways. Lightness of color seems a requisite for a stage position, unless a dark skin is offset by very great ability, as in the case of Aida Walker, one of the most graceful and charming women in musical comedy.

No record is kept of the number of colored teachers in the city's public schools, but each year Negro graduates from the normal college secure positions. These are found from

the kindergarten through the primary and
up to the highest grammar grade. The
colored girl with intellectual ability, particularly if she comes of an old New York
family, is apt to turn to teaching. Her
novitiate is long, but a permanent certificate secured, she is sure of a good salary,
increasing with her years of service, and
ending in a pension. This path of security
has perhaps tended to keep New York colored girls from going into other lines of
work. I have not yet found one who has
graduated from a university. Pratt Institute and the Teachers' College have colored
normal students, but they are usually from
the South or West, not New Yorkers born.

Philanthropy is opening up important lines
of opportunity to the Negro woman in New
York. In 1903, a colored graduate nurse
secured an interview with the Secretary of
the New York Charity Organization Society,
and so ably presented to him the need of
Negro visitors among Negroes that she was
appointed visiting nurse for the colored sick
who came under the notice of the Society.
In time the position changed into that of a

colored district visitor, other colored nurses
entering in numbers into district nursing
work.   In 1910, three nurses were employed
by the Nurses' Settlement, two by the Association for Improving the Condition of the
Poor of Manhattan, and two by the District
Nursing Association of Brooklyn.   With increased knowledge of the sickness and suffer-
ing amid the Negro poor, and of their need
of proper care in their homes, the number of
these nurses will doubtless increase.   Colored
women rank high among the trained nurses
of New York.

Other philanthropic work lately has been
undertaken by Negro women in New York.
In 1910, besides the nurses of whom we have
spoken, there were at the head of societies in
salaried positions, two settlement workers,
two matrons of day nurseries, two matrons of
homes in which much social work was carried
on, many employees in colored orphan
asylums, a teacher of domestic science in a
home-keeping flat, a traveller's aid visitor, a
playground instructor, besides workers in
various religious organizations.   This does
not include the many colored women doing

social and recreation work in the public schools and on the city's playgrounds. Indeed, the difficulty in New York is to secure trained colored women for philanthropic work, the Negro's attitude still being that of the great majority of white women a few years ago, that love for children and a sentimental kindness constitute the requisites for work among the poor. But the school of experience is training workers, and as the schools of philanthropy of New York, Boston, and Chicago also graduate colored students, we shall have in the North the intelligent, trained workers whom we need.

The little kindergarten girl who, with head erect, walked past the jeering line of boys to the green trees and soft grass of the park has her counterpart in many young women of New York. In 1909, a colored girl graduated from one of the city's dental colleges, the first woman of her race to take this degree in the state. From the first her success was remarkable. Colored girls with ability and steady purpose and dogged determination have won success in clerical and business work; but the last large and efficient group is that classified in the census under mechanical and manufacturing pursuits: the dressmakers, seamstresses, milliners.

Colored women have always been known as good sewers, and recently they have studied at their trade in some of the best schools. From 1904 to 1910, the Manhattan Trade School graduated thirty-four colored girls in dressmaking, hand sewing, and novelty making. The public night school on West Forty-sixth Street, under its able colored principal, Dr. W. L. Bulkley, since 1907, has educated hundreds of women in sewing, dressmaking, millinery, and artificial flower-making. While the majority of the pupils have taken the courses for their private use, a large minority are entering the business world. They meet with repeated difficulties; white girls refuse to work in shops with them, private employers object to their color, but they have, nevertheless, made creditable progress. The census reports the number of Negro dressmakers to have quadrupled in the United States from 1890 to 1900. Something comparable to this increase in dressmaking and allied trades has taken place among the Negroes of New York, and it has come through education and persistence, and the increase of trade among the colored group itself. Numbers of these dressmakers and milliners earn a livelihood, though often a scanty one, from the patronage of the people of their own race.

But despite her efforts and occasional successes, the colored girl in New York meets with severer race prejudice than the colored man, and is more persistently kept from attractive work. *She gets the job that the white girl does not want.* It may be that the white girls want the wrong thing, and that the jute mill and tobacco shop and flower factory are more dangerous to health and right living than the mistress's kitchen, but she knows her mind, and follows the business that brings her liberty of action when the six o'clock whistle blows. What she desires for herself, however, she refuses to her colored neighbor. Occasionally an employer objects to colored girls, but the Manhattan Trade School repeatedly, in trying to place its graduates, has found that opposition to the Negro has come largely from the working girls. Race prejudice has even gone so far as to prevent a colored woman from receiving home work when it entailed her waiting in the same sitting-room with white women. Of course, this is not the universal attitude. In friendly talks with hundreds of New York's white women workers I have found the majority ready to accept the colored worker. Jewish girls are especially tolerant. They believe that good character and decent manners should count, not color; but an aggressive, combative minority is quite sure that no matter how well educated or virtuous she may be, no black woman is as good as a white one. So the few but belligerent aristocrats triumph over the many half-ashamed, timid democrats.

The shirtwaist makers' strike of 1910 was so profoundly important in its breaking down of feeling between nationalities, its union of all working women in a common cause, that the colored girl, while very slightly concerned in the strike itself, may profit by the more generous feeling it engendered. Certainly an entrance into store and workshop would be to her immense advantage. She needs the discipline of regular hours, of steady training, of order and system. She needs also to become part of a strong labor group, to share its working class ideal, to feel the weight of its moral opinion; instead of looking into the mirror of her wealthy mistress, she needs to reflect the aspirations of the strong, earnest women who toil.

Before bringing the story of the life of the New York colored working woman to a close, it may not be amiss to look closely at the discrimination practised against her, not only in her work, but in her daily life. The Negro comes North and finds himself half a man. Does the woman, too, come to be but half a woman? What is her status in the city to which she turns for opportunity and larger freedom?

Four years ago, within a few hours' time, two stories were told me, illustrative of the colored woman's status. Neither occurred in the city of New York, but both are indicative of its temper. The first I heard from a woman skilled in a difficult profession, a Canadian now residing in the United States, and the descendant of a fugitive slave. Her youthful companions had all been white, and while an African in the darkness of her skin and her musical voice, her rearing had been that of an Englishwoman. "Shortly after coming to New York, I went for the first time," she told me, "to a little resort on the Jersey coast. A board walk flanked the ocean, and on the other side were shops and places of amusement. Going out one morning with two companions, a colored man and woman, we turned into an enclosure to examine a gaily painted merry-go-round. The place was open to the public, and a few nursery maids with their charges were seated about. The man in our party, interested in the mechanism of the machine, went up to it and began to explain it to us. Quite suddenly a rough fellow, in charge of the place, walked over and called out, 'Get out of here! We don't allow niggers.' The attack, to me at least, was so overwhelming that I did not move at once. Thereupon I was again called 'nigger,' and ordered out.

"When I reached the beach, I asked my companions to leave me, and I sat on a bench looking upon the waves. After a time an old woman came to my side, and said a little timidly, 'What are you thinking about, dearie?' Looking in her face I saw that she feared that I would commit suicide. 'I am thinking,' I said turning to her, 'that I wish the ocean might rise up and drown every white person on the face of the earth.' 'Oh, you mustn't say that,' she cried horrified, and left me. After I cannot tell how many minutes or hours, I returned to my boarding-house, and then to my home in New York. I had had a great many white friends in my native home; I had played with them, eaten with them, slept with them. Now I destroyed their letters, and resolved never to know them again. That was my first affront in the United States, and while I have learned to feel somewhat differently, a little to discriminate, I can never forget that the white people in the North stand for the insult which was cast upon me."

On the evening of the same day I had learned of this happening, a man from a prominent college in New York State told me of a Negro classmate. "He was a pleasant, intelligent fellow from the South," he said, "and while I never knew him well, I was always glad to see him. One day, at commencement time, when we were all having our relatives about, he boarded my car with a young colored woman, evidently his sister. Without a thought I rose, lifted my hat, and gave her my seat. Never again shall I see such a look of gratitude as that which lighted up his face when he bowed in acknowledgment of my courtesy. It revealed the race question to me, and yet I had performed only the simplest act of a gentleman."

In these two incidents we see the undecided, perplexing position of the Negro woman in New York. Today she may be turned out of a public resort as a "nigger," tomorrow she may receive the dues of a gentlewoman. And since, while I write, I hear the cry of a class in the community who adjudge the expulsion necessary since the other course must lead at once to social equality, I make haste to add that the second story did not end in wedlock. As far as I have seen, it never does. Intermarriage of white and black in New York is so slight as to be a negligible quantity, but amalgamation between the two races is not uncommon. And this we may say with certainty, the man most blatant against the "nigger" in New York as all over the country is the man most ready to enter into illicit relationship with the woman whom he claims to despise. The raising of the hat to the colored woman brings a diminution in sexual immorality.

If the Negro civilization of New York is to be lifted to a higher level, the white race must consistently play a finer and more generous part toward the colored woman. There are many inherent difficulties against which she must contend. Slavery deprived her of family life, set her to daily toil in the field, or appropriated her mother's instincts for the white child. She has today the difficult task of maintaining the integrity and purity of the home. Many times she has succeeded, often she has failed, sometimes she has not even tried. A vicious environment has strengthened her passions and degraded her from earliest girlhood.

Beyond any people in the city she needs all
the encouragement that philanthropy, that
human courtesy and respect, that the fellowship of the workers can give, — she needs her
full status as a woman.

CHAPTER VII

RICH AND POOR

OF the many nations and races that dwell in New York none, with the exception of the Chinese, is so aloof from us in its social life as the Negro. The childish recollection of an old school friend, recently related to me, well illustrates this. Across the way from where she lived there was a house occupied by a family of mulattoes. They were the quietest and least obtrusive people on the block, and the wife, who was known to be very beautiful, on the rare occasions when she left her home, was always veiled. The husband was little seen, and the child, a shy boy, never played on the street. For years the family lived aloof from their neighbors, the subject of hushed and mysterious questioning.

Probably had one of the white women dropped in some day to say good-morning

or to borrow a recipe book, the mystery
would have been wholly dispelled, — a pity
surely for the children. Few of New York's
citizens are so American as the colored, few
show so little that is unusual or picturesque.
The educated Italian might have in his
home some relic of his former country, the
Jew might show some symbol of his religion; but the Negro, to the seeker of the
unusual, would seem commonplace. The
colored man in New York has no associations with his ancient African home, no
African traditions, no folk lore. The days
of slavery he wishes completely to forget,
even to the loss of his exquisite plantation
music. He is ambitious to be conventional
in his manners, his customs, striving as far
as possible to be like his neighbor — a dis-
tinctly American ambition. In consequence,
after indicating the lines along which he has
achieved economic success, one finds little
to describe in the lives of the well-to-do
that will be of interest. And yet this sketch
would be open to criticism if, after so long
a survey of the working class, it gave no
space to those Negroes who have achieved

a fair degree of wealth and leisure; and perhaps the very recital of the likeness of these people to those about them may be of importance, for the great mass of white Americans are like a vivacious Kentuckian of my acquaintance, who, on learning something of a well-to-do Negro family, assured me that she knew less of such people than she did of the Esquimaux.

Mr. William Archer, in his book, "Through Afro-America," describes a round of visits to southern Negro homes, where, with touching pride, his hostesses show their material wealth, or rather the material wealth of their race as embodied in drawing-room, dining-room, and bedroom. There seemed to be nothing remarkable about the rooms unless their very existence was remarkable. So the interiors of colored homes in New York would reveal nothing to mark them from the homes of their neighbors, save perhaps the universal presence of some musical instrument. In Brooklyn, the Bronx, and in the Jersey suburbs, Negroes buy and rent houses, sometimes with a few of their race in close proximity, sometimes with white neigh-

bors only on the block. Brooklyn seems
always to have shown less race antagonism
than Manhattan (where, indeed, anything
but the apartment is beyond the pocket-
book of people of modest means), and it
has been in Brooklyn for the past three
generations that the well-to-do colored families with their children have chiefly been
found.

Much pleasant hospitality and entertainment take place behind these modest doors.
Visitors are common, relatives from the east
and west and south, and little dinner and
supper parties are numerous. If church discipline does not interfere, the women have
their afternoons of whist, and despite church
discipline, dancing is very common, few entertainments proving successful without it.
To play well upon some musical instrument
is almost a universal accomplishment, and,
as with the Germans, families and friends
meet the oftener for this harmonious bond.

The social life of the well-to-do colored
family generally centres about the church,
and with a regularity unusual among the
white people, father and mother and chil-

dren attend the Sunday and week-day meetings.   Colored society is also at the period
of the bazaar and fair, the concert and
dramatic entertainment.   Money is raised
by this means for the church, the private
charity, or to supplement the dues of the
mutual benefit society.   There are a number
of Negroes in the different large cities who
support themselves by concerts and readings,
appearing at benefits in the North and
South, where they receive a third or a half of
the receipts.   Amateur performances are also
common.   A young New York college man,
one winter evening, saw two refined, remark-
ably well-dressed colored women turn in at
the entrance of the Grand Central Palace.
Purchasing a ticket for the benefit, as it
proved, of a colored day nursery (the entertainment netted $2300), he followed them
to find himself in the Afro-American social
world.   For while the amateur dancing
and singing upon the stage were pretty
and attractive, the young man was far more
interested in the audience.   "And the dis-
appointing thing about it," he remarked
in telling of it afterwards, "was that they

were exactly like other people." To use the newspaper phrase, "there was no 'story.'" They were a group of Americans, trained in the social conventions of their own land.

There are many secret and benefit societies among the Negroes in New York. The Masons have nine meeting places; the Elks, ten lodges. The Odd Fellows have twenty-two places of meeting. The United Order of True Reformers, a strong Negro organization in the South, where it conducts large business enterprises, has forty-four head-quarters in church and hall and private house, where meetings are held twice a month. Many benefit societies are closely associated with the churches. Colored men and women are very busy with their multitudinous church and society and benefit meetings. I remember once attending an evening service at a colored church when the minister preached the sermon to the benefit orders of St. Luke's and the Galilean Fishermen. The officers, some of them carrying spears with blue and red and white trimmings, marched down the aisle and took their seats at the front of the pulpit.

Their leader was in purple, wearing a huge badge like a breastplate with yellow and green stones. The women, equally prominent with the men, were dressed one in yellow with green over it, and broad purple bands, two in white with golden crowns. The pageant was very pretty, even beautiful, but too artless in its simple enjoyment of color and display for the conventional society of New York, and the colored "four hundred" were not in it.

Who are the four hundred in New York's colored society? An outsider would be very bold who should attempt to answer. Twenty-five years ago the New Yorker born, especially the descendant of some prominent anti-slavery worker, would have held foremost social position. The taint of slavery was far removed from these people, who looked with scorn upon arrivals from the South. Many were proud of their Indian blood, and told of the freedom that came to their black ancestors who married Long Island Indians. But these old New York colored families, sometimes bearing historic Dutch and English names, have diminished in size and importance as have the old white families beside them. The younger generation has gone west, or has died and left no issue. And into the city has come a continual stream of Southerners and more recently West Indians, some among them educated, ambitious men and women, full of the energy and determination of the immigrant who means to attain to prominence in his new home. These new-comers occupy many of the pulpits, are admitted to the bar, practise medicine, and become leaders in politics, and their wives are quite ready to take a prominent part in the social world. They meet the older residents, and the various groups intermingle, though not without some friction. Like a country village, the New York Negro social world knows the happenings of its neighbors, gossips over their shortcomings, rejoices, though with something of jealousy, over their successes, and has its cliques, its many leaders, but also its broad-minded spirits who strive to bring the whole village life into harmony.

As we have learned from a study of the

occupational life of the Negro, the majority of men and women of means are in the professional class, or in the city or federal service. Such positions do not carry with them large incomes, and remembering the high cost of living in New York, and the exorbitant rental paid by black men, we can see that, gauged by the white man's standard, the Negro with his two or three or four thousand dollars a year is poor. Yet with his very limited income the demands upon him are enormous. In the first place, he must educate his children, and this means a large expenditure, for only in the technical schools or the college can his boy or girl be prepared for a successful career. The white boy may find some business firm that will give him a chance of advancement, but the colored boy must receive such an education as shall fit him to start an enterprise by himself, unless he enters public service. So the trade or professional school or college absorbs the savings of many years.

The church is another large recipient of the Negro's slender means. Watching the dimes and quarters drop into the contribu-

tion plate as the dark-faced congregation
files past the pulpit on a Sunday evening,
one wonders whether any other people in
America willingly give so large an amount
of their income to their religious organizations. And not only will money be requested
for the church's need, but special offerings
will be given to home and foreign mission work. In 1907, the African Methodist
Church alone raised $36,000 for home and for-
eign missions. The Baptists raised $44,000.
Educational work demands a share: the African Methodists support twenty schools, the
African Zion twelve, and the Negro Baptists
one hundred and twenty. The other de-
nominations do their share, and the Negroes
also give to the schools conducted by white
churches for their people. This money comes
from all over the country, and the well-to-do
New York Negro must contribute his part.

Home charities also help to drain the
Negro's purse. Manhattan and Brooklyn
have a number of colored philanthropies,
orphan asylums, old people's homes, rescue
missions, Young Men's and Young Women's
Christian Associations, and social settlements.

Some are supported entirely by white people, but the greater number receive some contributions from the colored, and a few are dependent for money upon that race alone. Thousands of dollars are raised yearly, among the well-to-do New York Negroes, for these institutions.

Yet, with all these various philanthropic activities, one too frequently hears that the Negro does not support his own charities. As though anything of the sort could be expected of him! A little time ago, in asking for money for settlement work among Negroes, I was asked in turn by the exquisitely dressed woman before me, whose furs and gown and jewels must have represented a year's salary of a school-teacher, the type of wealthy woman among the colored, why the well-to-do Negroes did not support the settlement themselves. No such question is asked when we demand money for work among the Italians or the Jews, who have incomparably larger means. Indeed, one may question whether the Negro is not too generous for the materialistic city of New York, whether his successes would not be

greater were he niggardly toward himself
and others. He lives well, dresses well,
enjoys a good play, strives to give every
advantage to his children, helps the poor of
his race. To hold his own today in this
civilization, he needs to be taught to seek
first riches, waiting until much treasure has
been laid up before he allows philanthropy
to draw upon his bank account.

The traveller to the British West Indies
finds three divisions among the inhabitants,
white, colored, and black, each group having a distinct social status. In the United
States, on the other hand, there are but two
groups, white and colored, or as the latter
is now more frequently designated, Negro,
the term thus losing its original meaning,
and becoming a designation for a race.
But while the white race usually makes no
social distinction between the light and the
dark Negro, classing all alike, social lines
are drawn within the color line. Years
ago these were more common than they are
now. Charles W. Chesnutt, the novelist,
tells some amusing and pathetic stories of
distinctions between colored and black. One

of his mulatto heroes, upon finding, as he thinks, that the congressman who is to call upon his daughter is a jet black Negro instead of the mulatto he was supposed to be, to prevent a breach of hospitality, invents a case of diphtheria in the family and quarantines the house, only to learn later, to his intense mortification, that he has committed a mistake of identification, and that the congressman is light after all. But this story belongs with the last generation. Black men, if they are distinguished citizens, can enter any colored society, and they not infrequently marry light wives. Success, a position of probity and importance, these are attributes that count favorably for the suitor, and as they are quite as often in the man of strong African lineage as in the mulatto, they gain the desired end.

Within this little colored world of a few thousand souls, a drop in the city's human sea, there is great upheaval and turmoil. The North is the Negro's centre for controversy regarding his rightful position in the commonwealth; and in the large cities, in Boston and Chicago, Philadelphia and New

York, the battle rages. The little society is
often divided into hostile camps regarding
party politics or the acceptance of a government position that brings the suspicion
of a bribe. Political, economic, educational
matters as they affect the black race, these
are the subjects that fill the mind of the
thoughtful colored man and woman.

In his "Souls of Black Folk," Dr. Du Bois
describes the white man's tactlessness when,
as always, he approaches the Negro with a
question regarding his race. But the Negro,
apart from his personal home affairs, im-
presses the outsider as having little else as
subject for conversation. World politics,
these concern him only as they affect the
race question. Australia is a country where
the government excludes Africans. England
rules in South Africa and has lately recognized the right of African disfranchisement.
Germany in Africa is cruel to black men.
The Latin people know no color line. At
home, the conflict of capital and labor is
important as the Negro wins or loses in the
economic struggle; the enfranchisement of
woman is wise or unwise as it would affect

Negro enfranchisement, one colored thinker
arguing against it since it would double the
white vote in the South where the Negro has
no political rights; literature is the poetry
of Dunbar, the writing of Washington and
Du Bois, the literature of the Negro question, and art is largely comprised in Tanner's paintings.

This picture should not imply that the
colored people of means are without the
possibility of wide culture and sympathy.
They are perhaps more sympathetic by
nature than the white people about them.
But each year, as the white American grows
increasingly conscious of race, as he argues
on racial differences, the Negro feels his
dark face, is sensitive to every disdainful
look, and separates himself from the people
about him and their problems.

There is a struggle against this. The
majority of white people have heard, in a
vague way, that there is a difference of
opinion in the Negro world; and again,
vaguely, that it takes the form of opposition
to Dr. Booker T. Washington and industrial
training. But the difference of opinion

among the Negroes is a difference of ideals,
and reaches far beyond the controversy of
industrial or cultural training, or the question of individual leadership. It is difficult
to formulate, inasmuch as few, if any,
Negroes hold logically to one ideal wholly
to the exclusion of the other. They cannot
be logical and live. But their division into
radical and conservative is too important to
omit; especially since, as we have seen, there
is nothing in their social life to distinguish
them from their neighbors; only in their
thoughts are they aloof from us — aliens
upon whose shoulders is the problem of a
race.

How can one explain these two ideals?
Roughly, they accept or reject segregation.
The first looks upon the black man in America, for many generations at least, as a race
apart. Recognizing this, the race must increasingly grow in self-efficiency. It must
run its own businesses, own its banks, its
groceries, its restaurants, have its dressmakers, milliners, tailors; it must establish
factories where it shall employ only colored
men and women; its children shall be brought

into the world by colored doctors, taught by colored teachers, buried by colored undertakers. Education, along industrial lines, shall help train the worker to this efficiency, and a proper race pride shall give him the patronage of the Negroes about him. When, as will of course happen in the majority of cases, the Negro works for the white man, he must consider himself and his race. He must not go out on strike when the white man strives for higher wages; he is justified, if he is willing to risk a broken head, in filling the place of the striking workman, for he has to look after his own concerns.

The second point of view resists segregation. It believes that the Negro should never cease to struggle against being treated as a race apart, that he should demand the privileges of a citizen, free access to all public institutions, full civil and political rights. As a workman, he should have the opportunity of other workmen, his training should be the training of his white neighbor, and in business and the professions he should strive to serve white as well as black. And just as in the battle-field he fights in a com-

mon cause with his white comrade, so in the
struggle for better working class conditions
he should stand by the side of the laborer,
regardless of race. Believing these things
and finding that America fails to meet his
demands, he thinks it should be his part to
struggle for his ideal, vigorously to protest
against discrimination, and never, compla-
cent, to submit to the position of inferiority.

As I have said, few men hold logically to
either of these ideals, and as that of acqui-
escence to present conditions is naturally
popular with the whites, who are themselves
responsible for discrimination, material success sometimes means a departure from the
aggressive to the submissive attitude. However, the whole question of the Negro as a
wage earner is yet scarcely understood by
this small professional and business class.
They are in turmoil, in a virile struggle,
harsh, bewildering, baffling.

"I cannot conceive what it would mean
not to be a Negro," a prominent New York
colored man once said to me. "The white
people think and feel so little; their life
lacks an absorbing interest."

This is the characteristic fact of the life of the well-to-do Negro in New York. He is not permitted to go through the city streets in easy comfort of body or mind. Some personal rebuff, some harsh word in newspaper or magazine, quickens his pulse and rouses him from the lethargy that often overtakes his comfortable white neighbor. Looking into the past of slavery, watching the coming generation, the most careless of heart is forced into serious questioning. A comfortable income and the intelligence to enjoy the culture of a great city do not bring to the Negro any smug self-satisfaction; only a greater responsibility toward the problem that moves through the world with his dark face.

Before turning to our last topic, the Negro and the Municipality, we ought to note two further characteristics of the Negro in New York.

There are certain statistics quoted by every writer upon the Negro, statistics of mortality and crime. We have noted these for the child, but not as yet for the Negroes as a whole. They have been left until this

point in our study that we may view them
in relation to what we have learned of the
Negro's economic condition and his environment.

Looking for criminal statistics first, we
find them difficult to obtain in New York.
The courts' reports do not classify by color,
but we can learn something from the census
enumeration of 1904 of the prisoners in the
New York County Penitentiary and the New
York County Workhouse. These are short
term offenders sent up from the city of New
York. The enumeration is as follows:

NEW YORK COUNTY PENITENTIARY (BLACKWELL'S ISLAND)

	Total	Males	Females	Per cent Total	Per cent Females
White	582	533	49	91.8	8.4
Colored	52	33	19	8.2	36.5

NEW YORK COUNTY WORKHOUSE

	Total	Males	Females	Per cent Total	Per cent Females
White	1126	870	256	96.5	22.7
Colored	41	12	29	3.5	70.7

In view of the proportion of Negroes to
whites in Manhattan, two per cent, we find

the percentage of colored prisoners high, but no higher than we expect when we remember that the Negro occupies the lowest plane in the industrial community, "the plane which everywhere supplies the jail, the penitentiary, the gallows." [1] But the very large percentage of crime among colored women calls for grave consideration. In the workhouse, imprisoned for fighting, for drunkenness, for prostitution, the colored women more than double in number the colored men. Here is a condition that we noted in the Children's Court records: an unduly large percentage of disorderly and depraved colored female offenders.

We have already touched upon the subject of morality among colored women. Various causes, some of which we have noted, go to the making up of this high percentage of crime. The Negroes themselves believe the basic cause to be their recent enslavement with its attendant unstable marriage and parental status. They point to the centuries of healthful home relationships among Amer-

[1] Quincy Ewing, "The Heart of the Race Problem," *Atlantic Monthly*, March, 1909.

icans and Europeans, and contrast them with
the thousands upon thousands of yearly
sales of slaves that but two generations ago
disrupted the Negro's attempts at family
life. With this heritage they believe that
it is inevitable that numbers of their women
should be slow to recognize the sanctity of
home and the importance of feminine virtue.

The mortality figures for the New York
Negro are more striking than the figures for
crime. In 1908 the death rate for whites in
the city was 16.6 in every thousand; for
colored (including Chinese), 28.9, almost
double the white rate. The Negroes' greatest excess over the white was in tuberculosis,
congenital debility, and venereal diseases as
the table on the following page shows.

The Negro's inherent weakness, his inability to resist disease, is a favorite topic
today with writers on the color question.
A high mortality is indeed a matter for grave
concern, but we may question whether these
figures show inherent weakness. If a new
disease attacks any group of people, it causes
terrible decimation, and tuberculosis and
venereal diseases, the white man's plagues,

have proved terribly destructive to the black
man. But recalling the conditions under
which the great majority of the colored race

New York, 1908.	White.	Colored.
Number of deaths from all causes per 1000 population	16.6	28.9
Number of deaths per 1000 deaths:		
Tuberculosis	136.	232.8
Pneumonia.........................	126	136.3
Diarrhœa and enteritis...............	91.8	79
Bright's disease	78.3	56.5
Heart disease	76.7	83.4
Cancer	45.5	24.8
Congenital debility	24.5	34.1
Diphtheria and croup	23.7	15.
Scarlet fever	19.	3.2
Typhoid	7.3	6.9
Venereal diseases	4.	13.4
All others	367.2	314.6
	1000.0	1000.0

lives in New York, the long hours of labor,
the crowded rooms, the insufficient food, we
find abundant cause for a high death rate.
For poverty and death go hand in hand, and
the proportion of Negroes in New York who
live in great poverty far exceeds the proportion of whites.[1]

[1] The statistician, Mr. I. B. Rubinow, in a discussion of

The students at Hampton Institute sing
an old plantation song that runs like this:

"If religion was a thing that money could buy,
The rich would live and the poor would die.
But my good Lord has fixed it so
The rich and the poor together must go."

Some of our rich men seem to have fixed
it with religion to escape from the condition
the poem describes, but it depicts a reality
in the Negro's life. Rich and poor, as we
saw when we left our old New Yorkers,
competent and inefficient, pure and diseased,
good and bad, all go together. Much of the
recent literature written by Negroes, and

high death rates (American Statistical Association, December,
1905) quotes the rate in five agricultural districts in a province
of Russia, districts inhabited by peasantry of a common stock.
With almost mathematical certainty, prosperity brings longer
life. He divides his peasants into six groups showing their
death rate as follows:

	Death Rate
Having no land	34.7
Less than 13.5 acres	32.7
13.5 to 40.5 acres	30.1
40.5 to 67.5 acres	25.4
67.5 acres to 135 acres	23.1
More than 135 acres	19.2

Mr. Rubinow suggests that the high Negro death rate
may be explained by noting the poorly paid occupations in
which the Negro engages.

especially that by Dr. Booker T. Washington, attempts to separate in the minds of the community the thrifty and prosperous colored men from the helpless and degraded; but the effort meets with a limited success. When we can have a statistical study of some thousands of the well-to-do Negroes compared with an equal number of well-to-do whites, we may find striking similarity. From my own observations I find that the well-to-do Negroes bear and rear children, refrain from committing crimes that put them into jail, and live to an old age with the same success as their white neighbors. But they get little credit for it. Willy-nilly, the strong, intellectual Negro is linked to his unfortunate fellow. Whether an increase in material prosperity will break this bond, or whether it will continue until it ceases to be a bond as humanity comes into its own, is a secret of the future. For today the song rings true, and the rich and the poor go together.

CHAPTER VIII

THE NEGRO AND THE MUNICIPALITY

A CAPRICIOUS mood, varying with the individual, considerate today and offensive tomorrow, this, as far as our observations have led us, has been New York's attitude toward the Negro. Is it possible to find any principle underlying this shifting position? The city expresses itself through the individual actions of its changing four millions of people, but also through its government, its courts of justice, its manifold public activities. Out of these various manifestations of the community's spirit can we find a Negro policy? Has New York any principle of conduct toward these her colored citizens? This question should be worth our consideration, for New York's attitude means its environmental influence, and helps determine for the newly arrived immigrant and the growing generation whether justice or intol-

195

erance shall mark their dealings with the black race.

The first matter of civic importance to the Negro, as to every other New York resident, is his position in the commonwealth; is he a participant in the government under which he lives, or a subject without political rights? The law since 1873 has been explicit on this matter, wiping out former property qualifications, and giving full manhood suffrage. Probably, even with a much larger influx of colored people, the city will never agitate this question again. Since the death of the Know-nothing Party, New York has ceased any organized attempt to lessen the power of the foreigner, and the growing cosmopolitan character of the population strengthens the Negro in his rights. Only in those states where the white population is homogeneous can Negro disfranchisement successfully take place.

With the vote the Negro has entered into politics and has maintained successful political organizations. The necessity of paying for rent and food out of eight or ten dollars a week is the Negro's immediate issue in

New York, and he tries to meet it by securing a congenial and more lucrative job. The city in 1910 showed some consideration for him in this matter. An Assistant District Attorney and an Assistant Corporation Counsel were colored, and scattered throughout the city departments were nine clerks making from $1200 to $1800 apiece, and a dozen more acting as messengers, inspectors, drivers, attendants, receiving salaries averaging $1275. Three doctors served the Board of Health, and there were six men on the police force (none given patrol duty), and one first grade fireman, while the departments of docks, parks, street cleaning, and water supply employed 470 colored laborers. Altogether 511 colored men figure among the city's employees.[1]

In her communal gifts the city acts toward the Negro with a fair degree of impartiality. At the public schools and libraries, the parks and playgrounds, the baths, hospitals, and, last, the almshouse, the blacks have equal rights with the whites. Occasionally indi-

[1] The total number of municipal employees is 55,006 — Negro employees, 511 — Percentage of Negro to whole, 0.9.

vidual public servants show color prejudice,
but again, occasionally, especial kindness
attends the black child. The rude treatment awaiting them, however, from other
visitors keeps many Negro children, and
men and women, from enjoying the city's
benefactions. Particularly is this true with
the public baths and with some of the playgrounds. The employment by the city of
at least one colored official in every neighborhood where the Negroes are in great
numbers would do much to remedy this
condition.

One department of the city might be cited
as having been an exception to the rule of
reasonably fair treatment to the colored
man. Harshness, for no cause but his black
face, has been too frequently bestowed upon
the Negro by the police. This has been
especially noticeable in conflicts between
white and colored, when the white officer,
instead of dealing impartially with offenders,
protected his own race.

There have been two conflicts between the
whites and Negroes in New York in recent
years, the first in 1900, on the West Side, in

the forties, the second in 1905, on San Juan
Hill. Each riot was local, representing no
wide-spread excitement comparable to the
draft riots of 1863, and in each case the police
might easily in the beginning have stopped all
fighting. Instead, they showed themselves
ready to aid, even to instigate the conflict.

The riot of 1900 was caused by the death
of a policeman at the hands of a Negro.
The black man declared that he was defending his life, but the officer was popular, and
after his funeral riots began. Black men ran
to the police for protection, and were thrown
back by them into the hands of the mob.[1]

The riot of 1905 commenced on San Juan
Hill one Friday evening in July with a
fracas between a colored boy and a white
peddler; both races took a hand in the matter
until the side streets showed a rough scram-
bling fight. Saturday and Sunday were
comparatively quiet; men, black and white,
stood on street corners and scowled at one
another, but nothing further need have
occurred, had each race been treated with

[1] "Story of the Riot," published by Citizens Protective
League.

justice. The police, however, instead of keeping the peace, angered the Negroes, urged on their enemies, and by Monday night found that they had helped create a riot, this time bitter and dangerous. Over-zealous to proceed against the "niggers," officers rushed into places frequented by peaceable colored men, whom they placed under arrest. Dragging their victims to the station-house they beat them so unmercifully that before long many needed to be handed over to another city department — the hospital. Little question was made as to guilt or innocence, and some of the worst offenders, colored as well as white, were never brought to justice.[1] "If," as a colored preacher whose church was the centre of the storm district pointed out, "the police would only differentiate between the good and the bad Negroes, and not knock on the head every colored man they saw in a riot, we should be quite satisfied. As it is, there is no safety for any Negro in this part of the city at any time."[2]

[1] New York *Age*, July 27, 1905.
[2] New York *Tribune*, July 24, 1905.

The result of these two riots was the bringing to justice of one policeman and the
placing of a humane and tactful captain on
San Juan Hill. But for some time the colored
man felt little protection in the Department
of Police, finding that he was liable to arrest
and clubbing for a trivial offence. Often
the officer's club fell with cruel force. This,
however, was before the administration of
Mayor Gaynor, who has commanded humane
treatment, and the brutal clubbing of the
New York Negro has now ceased.

From the police one turns naturally to the
courts. What is their attitude toward the
Negro offender? Is there any race prejudice,
or do black and white enjoy an impartial and
judicial hearing?

As the Negro comes before the magistrates
of the city courts, he learns to know that
judges differ greatly in their conceptions of
justice. To the Southerner, let us say from
Richmond, where the black man is arrested
for small offences and treated with considerable roughness and harshness, New York
courts seem lenient.[1] To the West Indian,

[1] A southern student says, "The Negro in Richmond is

accustomed to British rule, justice in New York is noticeable for its variability, the likelihood that if it is severe tonight, it will be generous tomorrow.

"Three months," the listener at court hears given as sentence to a respectable-looking colored servant girl who has begged to be allowed to return to her place which she has held for five years. "I never was up for drinking before," she pleads; "I have learnt my lesson; please give me a chance; I will not do this again."

"What should you two be fighting for?" another judge, another morning, says to two very battered women, one white and one colored, who come before him in court. And talking kindly to both, but with greater seriousness to the Irish offender, his own countrywoman, he sends them away with a reprimand.

How much of this unequal treatment comes arrested for small offences and fined in the city courts. He is treated with considerable roughness and harshness in his punishment for these offences. It looks as though he were being imposed upon as an individual of the lower strata of society. But the Negro responds so impulsively to what appeals, that constant fear, dread, and impressiveness of the police act well as resistants to temptations."

from color prejudice or caprice or temperament, the Negro is unable to decide, but he soon learns one curious fact: while his black skin marks him as inheriting Republican politics, it is the Democratic magistrate, the Tammany henchman whose name is a byword to the righteous, who is the more lenient when he has committed a trifling offence.

"Didn't I play craps with the nigger boys when I was a kid?" one of these well-known politicians says, "and am I going back on the poor fellows now?" Of course, the Negro is assured such men only want his vote, but he believes real sympathy actuates the Tammany leader, who is too busy to bother whether the man before him is black or white. The reformer, on the other hand, big with dignity, at times makes him vastly uncomfortable as he lectures upon the Negro problem from the eminence of the superior race.

But whether Republican or Democrat, the Negro learns that it is well to have a friend at court; that helplessness is the worst of all disabilities, worse than darkness of skin or poverty. So he soon becomes acquainted with his local politician, and if his friend is in trouble, or his wife or son is locked up, pounds vigorously at the politician's door. It may be midnight, but the man of power will dress, and together they will turn from the dark tenement hall into the lighted street and on to the police-station or magistrate's court to seek release for the offender. That too often the gravity of the offence weighs little in the securing of lenient treatment is part of the muddle of New York justice. The Negro finds that he has taken the most direct way to secure relief.

As far as we have followed, we have found the municipality of New York generally ready to treat her black citizens with the same justice or injustice with which she treats her whites. Exceptions occur, but she does not often draw the color line. Perhaps, in this connection, it might be well to stop a moment and see what return the black man makes, whether by his vote he helps secure to the city honest and efficient government.

Walking through a Negro quarter on elec-

tion day, the most careful search fails to reveal any such far-sighted altruism. With a
great majority of colored voters the choice of
a municipal candidate is based on the argument of a two-dollar bill or the promise of a
job, combined with the sentiment, decreas-
ing every year, for the Republican Party —
the party that once helped the colored man
and, he hopes, may help him again. The
public standing of the mayoralty candidate,
his ability to choose wise heads of departments, the building of new subways, the
ownership of public utilities, these are unimportant issues. The matter of immediate moment is what this vote is going to
mean to the black voter himself.

Such a selfish and unpatriotic attitude,
not unknown perhaps to white voters, leads
some of our writers and reformers to doubt
the value of universal manhood suffrage.
Mr. Ray Stannard Baker tells us that the
Negro and the poor white in New York,
through their venality, are practically without a vote. "While the South is disfran-
chising by legislation," he says, "the North
is doing it by cash." "What else is the

meaning of Tammany Hall and the boss and machine system in other cities?"[1] New York's noted ethical culture teacher argues against agitation for woman's suffrage on the ground that so many of those who now have the vote do not know how to use it. But looking closely at these unaltruistic citizens, we see that after all they are putting the ballot to its primary use, the protection of their own interests. The Negro in New York has one vital need, steady, decent work. He dickers and plays with politics to get as much of this as he can. It is very insufficient relief for an intolerable situation, but it is partial relief. In another city, Atlanta for instance, he might find education the most important civic gift for which to strive. Atlanta is a fortunate city to choose for an example of the power of the suffrage, for since the Negro's loss of the vote in Georgia, educational funds have been turned chiefly to white schools, and 5,000 colored children are without opportunities for public education. 1885 saw the last school building erected for Negroes, the result of a bargain

[1] Ray Stannard Baker, "Following the Color Line," p. 269.

between the colored voters and the prohibi-
tionists.[1] Should a colored teacher in New
York be refused her certificate, a colored
consumptive be denied a place in the city's
hospital, a colored child meet with a rebuff
in the city park, the colored citizen would

[1] The following story of Athens, Georgia, told by a North-
erner teaching in the South, illustrates this point. "The city
of Athens was planning to inaugurate a public school system,
and also wished to 'go dry.' It made a proposal to the colored voters promising that if their combined vote would
carry the city, two schools should be built, of equal size and
similar structure for each race. I visited Athens shortly after
the two buildings were built, and I found two beautiful brick
buildings very similar in all their appointments. At an inter-
val of several years I again visited the little city and again
spent an hour in the same brick school-house of the colored
folk.

"At my third visit, I found my colored friends occupying
a wooden structure on the edge of the city, and not only incon-
veniently located, but much less of a building than the one
hitherto occupied. Upon inquiry I found that in the growth
of the school population of the whites, it was cheaper to seize
the building formerly occupied by the colored children, and to
build for them a cheap wooden structure on the outskirts of
the town.

"The colored school was still occupying this inadequate
building at my visit this last September, 1909. A second
wooden structure has been added to the colored equipment
on the east side of the town."

This story of the Athenians well illustrates what will be
done when the Negro counts for something politically, and
also what may be undone if his value as a political asset is
reduced.

find his vote an important means of redress.
Then, too, while there are so many men to
buy, it is important to have a vote to sell,
lest the other citizens secure the morning's
bargains. Venality in high and low places
will not disappear until we are dominated
by the ideal of social, not individual advancement. Before that time, it is well for the
weak that they are able, at least in the
political field, to bargain with the strong.

The importance to the Negro of the vote
is quickly appreciated when we consider New
York's attitude unofficially expressed. With
the franchise behind him the colored man
can secure for himself and his children
the municipality's advantages of education,
health, amusement, philanthropy. He is
here a citizen, a contributor to the city
treasury, if not directly as a taxpayer, as a
worker and renter. But as a private individual, seeking to use the utilities managed
by other private individuals, he continually encounters race discrimination. Private
doors are closed, and were the state not so
wealthy and generous, disabilities still graver
than at present would follow.

A few examples will show the condition. A Negro applies by letter for admission to an automobile school, and is accepted; but on appearing with his fee his color debars his entrance. Carrying the case to court, the complaint is dismissed on the ground that the law which forbade exclusion from places of education on account of race and color is applicable only to public schools. Private institutions may do as they desire.

Again, a colored man tries to get a meal. At the first restaurant he is told that all the tables are engaged; at the next no one will serve him. Fearful of further rebuffs, he has to turn to the counter of a railway station. He wants to go to the theatre. Like Tommy Atkins, he is sent to the gallery or round the music halls. The white barber whose shop he enters will not shave him; and when night comes, he searches a long time before the hotel appears that will give him a bed. The sensitive man, still more the sensitive woman, often finds the city's attitude difficult to endure.

American Negroes have become familiar

with racial lines, but the foreigner of African descent, a visitor to the city, meets with rebuffs that fill him with surprise as well as rage. Haytians and South Americans, men of continental education and wide culture, have been ordered away as "niggers" from restaurant doors, and at the box office of the theatre refused an orchestra seat. English Negroes from the West Indies, men and women of character and means, learn that New York is a spot to be avoided, and cross the ocean when they wish to taste of city life. In short, the stranger of Negro descent, if he be rash of temper, hurls anathemas at the villainously mannered Americans; or, if he be good-natured, shrugs his shoulders and counts New York a provincial settlement of four million people.

Northern Negroes believe this discrimination in public places against the black man to be increasing in New York. One, who came here fifteen years ago, tells of the simple and adequate test by which he learned that he had reached the northern city. Born in South Carolina, as he attained manhood he desired larger self-expression, broader human relations — he wanted "to be free," as he again and again expressed it. So leaving the cotton fields he started one morning to walk to New York. After a number of days he entered a large city and, uncertain in his geography, decided that this was his journey's end. "I'll be free here," he thought, and opening the door of a brightly lighted restaurant started to walk in. The white men at the tables looked up in astonishment, and the proprietor, laying his hand on the youth's shoulder, invited him, in strong southern accent, to go into the kitchen. "I reckon I'm not North yet," the Negro said, smiling a bright, boyish smile. Interested in his visitor's appearance, the proprietor took him into another room, gave him a good supper, and talked with him far into the night, urging the advantages of his staying in the South. But the youth shook his head, and the next morning trudged on. At length he reached a rushing city, tumultuous with humanity, and entering an eating-house was served a meal. To him it was almost a sacrament. He belonged not to a race but to humanity. He tasted the freedom

of passing unnoticed. But it is doubtful
if the same restaurant would serve him
today.

Color lines, on these matters of entertainment as on others, are not hard and fast. A
few hotels, chiefly those frequented by Latin
peoples, receive colored guests; and while
the foreign Negro meets with rudeness, he
is rebuffed less than the native. "I can't
get into that place as a southern darky," a
black man laughingly says, pointing to a
fashionable restaurant, "I'll be the Prince
of Abyssinia." But as Prince or American
his status is shifting and uncertain; here,
preeminently, he is half a man.

Discrimination against any man because of
his color is contrary to the law of the state.
After the fifteenth amendment became a
law, New York passed a civil rights bill,
which as it stands, re-enacted in 1909, is
very explicit. All persons within the jurisdiction of the state are entitled to the accommodation of hotels, restaurants, theatres,
music halls, barbers' shops, and any person
refusing such accommodation is subject to
civil and penal action. The offence may

be punished by fine or imprisonment or both.[1]

In 1888, the attempt to exclude three colored men from a skating-rink at Binghamton, N. Y., led to a suit against the owner of the rink, and his conviction. The case[2]

[1] Civil Rights Law, State of New York. Chapter 14 of the Laws of 1909, being Chapter 6 of the Consolidated Laws.

"Article 4. — Equal rights in places of public amusement.

"Section 40. — All persons within the jurisdiction of this state shall be entitled to the full and equal accommodations, advantages, facilities, and privileges of inns, restaurants, hotels, eating houses, bath houses, barber shops, theatres, music halls, public conveyances on land and water, and all other places of public accommodation or amusement, subject only to the conditions and limitations, established by the law and applicable alike to all citizens.

"Section 41. — Penalty for violation. Any person who shall violate any of the provisions of the foregoing section by denying to any citizen, except for reasons applicable alike to all citizens of every race, creed and color, and regardless of race, creed and color, the full enjoyment of any of the accommodations, advantages, facilities or privileges in said section enumerated, or by aiding or inciting such denial, shall, for every such offence, forfeit and pay a sum not less than one hundred dollars nor more than five hundred dollars to the person aggrieved thereby, to be recovered in a court of competent jurisdiction in the County where said offence was committed, and shall also, for every such offence, be deemed guilty of a misdemeanor, and upon conviction thereof shall be fined not less than one hundred dollars nor more than five hundred dollars, or shall be imprisoned not less than thirty days nor more than ninety days, or both such fine and imprisonment."

[2] People vs. King, 110 N. Y., 418, 1888.

reached the Court of Appeals, where the constitutionality of the civil rights bill was upheld. "It is evident," said Justice Andrews in his decision, "that to exclude colored people from places of public resort on account of their race is to fix upon them a brand of inferiority, and tends to fix their position as a servile and dependent people."

But despite the law and precedent, the civil rights bill is violated in New York. Occasionally colored men bring suit, but the magistrate dismisses the complaint. Usually the evidence is declared insufficient. A case of a colored man refused orchestra seats at a theatre is dismissed on the ground that not the proprietor but his employees turned the man away. A keeper of an ice-cream parlor, wishing to prevent the colored man from patronizing him, charges a Negro a dollar for a ten-cent plate. The customer pays the dollar, keeps the check, and brings the case to court. Ice-cream parlors are then declared not to come under the list of places of public entertainment and amusement. A bootblack refuses to polish the shoes of a Negro, and the court decides that a bootblack-stand is not a place of public accommodation, and refusal to shine the shoes of a colored man does not subject its proprietor to the penalties imposed by the law.[1] This last case was carried to the Court of Appeals, and the adverse judgment has led many of the thoughtful colored men of the city to doubt the value of attempting to push a civil rights suit. Litigation is expensive, and money spent in any personal rights case that attacks private business, whether the plaintiff be white or colored, is usually wasted. The civil rights law is on the books, and the psychological moment may arrive to insist successfully on its enforcement.

If there is an increase in discrimination against the Negro in New York solely because of his color, it is a serious matter to the city as well as to the race. Every community has its social conscience built up of slowly accumulated experiences, and it cannot without disaster lose its ideal of justice or generosity. New York has never been tender to its people, but it has a rough hospitality, what Stevenson describes as "uncivil

[1] Burke *vs*. Bosso, 180 N. Y., 341, 1905.

kindness," and welcomes new-comers with a
friendly shove, bidding them become good
Americans. After the war, the Negro entered more than formerly into this general
welcome. He was unnoticed, allowed to go
his way without questioning word or stare,
the position which every right-minded man
and woman desires. But today New York
has become conscious that he is dark-skinned,
and her attitude affects her growing children.
"I never noticed colored people," an old
abolitionist said to me, "I never realized
there were white and black until, when a boy
of twelve, I entered a church and found
Negroes occupying seats alone in the gallery." As New York returns to the gallery
seats, her boys and girls return to conscious-
ness of color and, from fisticuffs at school,
move on to the race riots upon the streets
with bullets among the stones.

The municipality, as we have seen, treats
the Negro on the whole with justice; its
standard is higher than the standard of the
average citizen. It cherishes the ideal of democracy, and strives for impartiality toward
its many nationalities and races. And the

New York Negro in his turn does not allow his liberties to be tampered with without protest. But the New York citizen can hardly be described as friendly to the Negro. What catholicity he has is negative. He fails to give the black man a hearty welcome. "Do you know where I stayed the four weeks of my first trip abroad?" a colored clergyman once asked me. I refused to make a guess. "Well," he said a little shamefacedly, "it was in Paris. Paris may be a wicked city — any city has wickedness if you want to look for it — but I found it a place of kindliness and good-will. Every one seemed glad to be courteous, to assist me in my stumbling French, to show me the way on omnibus or boat, or through the difficult streets. It was so different from America; I was never wanted in the southern city of my youth. In Paris I was welcome."

"How is it in New York?" I asked.

"In New York?" He stopped to consider. "In New York I am tolerated."

CHAPTER IX

CONCLUSION

A NEW little boy came two years ago into our story-book world. When Miss North, taking Ezekiel by the hand, led him into her school-room,[1] we met a child full of what we call temperament; dreaming quaint stories, innocently friendly, anxious to please for affection's sake, in his queer, unconscious way something of a genius. We saw his big musing eyes looking out upon a world in which his teacher stood serene and reasoning, but a little cold like her name; his friend, Miss Jane, kind and very practical; his employer, Mr. Rankin, amused and contemptuous; all watching him with the impersonal interest with which one might view a new species in the animal world. For Ezekiel, unlike our other story-book boys, had a double being, he was first Ezekiel Jordan, a

[1] Lucy Pratt, "Ezekiel."

218

little black boy, and second, a Representative of the Negro Race.

Ezekiel was too young to understand his position, but the white world about him never forgot it. When he arrived late to school, he was a dilatory representative; when, obliging little soul, he promised three people to weed their gardens all the same afternoon, he was a prevaricating representative. He never happened to steal ice-cream from the hoky-poky man or to play hookey, but if he had, he would have been a thieving and lazy representative. Always he was something remote and overwhelming, not a natural growing boy.

Ezekiel's position is that of each Negro child and man and woman in the United States today. I think we have seen this as we have reviewed the position of the race in New York; indeed, the very fact of our attempting such a review is patent that we see and feel it. We white Americans do not generalize concerning ourselves, we individualize, leaving generalizations to the chance visitor, but we generalize continually concerning colored Americans; we classify and measure and pass judgment, a little more with each succeeding year.

Now if we are going to do this, let us be fair; let us try as much as possible to dismiss prejudice, and to look at the Ezekiels entering our school of life, with the same impartiality and the same understanding sympathy with which we look upon our own race. And if we are to place them side by side with the whites, let us be impartial, not cheating them out of their hard-earned credits, or condemning them with undue severity. Let us try, if we can, to be just.

When we begin to make this effort to judge fairly our colored world, we need to remember especially two things: First, that we cannot yet measure with any accuracy the capability of the colored man in the United States, because he has not yet been given the opportunity to show his capability. If we deny full expression to a race, if we restrict its education, stifle its intellectual and æsthetic impulses, we make it impossible fairly to gauge its ability. Under these circumstances to measure its achievements with the more favored white race is unreasonable and unjust, as unreasonable as to measure against a man's a disfranchised woman's capabilities in directing the affairs of a state.[1]

The second thing is difficult for us to remember, difficult for us at first to believe; that we, dominant, ruling Americans, may not be the persons best fitted to judge the Negro. We feel confident that we are, since we have known him so long and are so familiar with his peculiarities; but in moments of earnest reflection may it not occur to us that we have not the desire or the imagination to enter into the life emotions of others? "We are the intellect and virtue of the airth, the cream of human natur', and the flower of moral force," Hannibal Chollup

[1] "The world of modern intellectual life is in reality a white man's world. Few women and perhaps no blacks have entered this world in the fullest sense. To enter it in the fullest sense would be to be in it at every moment from the time of birth to the time of death, and to absorb it unconsciously and consciously, as the child absorbs language. When something like this happens we shall be in a position to judge of the mental efficiency of women and the lower races. At present we seem justified in inferring that the differences in mental expression between the higher and lower races and between men and women are no greater than they should be in view of the existing differences in opportunity." W. I. Thomas, "Sex and Society," p. 312.

still says, and glowers at the stranger who dares to suggest a different standard from his own. Hannibal Chollup and his ilk are ill-fitted to measure the refinements of feeling, the differences in ideals among people.

This question of our fitness to sit in the judgment seat must come with grave insistence when we read carefully the literature published in this city of New York within the past two years. Our writers have assumed such pomposity, have so revelled in what Mr. Chesterton calls "the magnificent buttering of one's self all over with the same stale butter; the big defiance of small enemies," as to make their conclusions ridiculous. Ezekiel entering their school is at once pushed to the bottom of the class, while the white boy at the head, Hannibal Chollup's descendant, sings a jubilate of his own and butters himself so copiously as to be as shiny as his English cousin, Wackford Squeers. Then the writer, the judge, begins. Ezekiel is shown as the incorrigible boy of the school. He is a lazy, good-for-nothing vagabond. Favored with the chance to exercise his muscles twelve hours a day for a disinterested employer, he fails to appreciate his opportunity. He is diseased, degenerate. His sisters are without chastity, every one, polluting the good, pure white men about them. He is a rapist, and it is his criminal tendencies that are degrading America. The pale-faced ones of his family steal into white society, marry, and insinuate grasping, avaricious tendencies into the noble, generous men of white blood, causing them to cheat in business and to practise political corruption. In short there is nothing evil that Ezekiel is not at the bottom of. Sometimes, poor little chap, he tries to sniffle out a word, to say that his family is doing well, that he has an uncle who is buying a home, and a rich cousin in the undertaking business, but such extenuating circumstances receive scant attention, and we are not surprised to find, the class dismissed, that Ezekiel and the millions whom he represents, are swiftly shuffled off the earth, victims of "disease, vice, and profound discouragement."

Now this is not an exaggerated picture of much that has recently been printed in newspaper and magazine, and does it not make us feel the paradox that if we are to judge the Negro fairly, we must not judge him at all, so little are we temperamentally capable of meeting the first requirement?

"My brother Saxons," says Matthew Arnold, "have a terrible way with them of wanting to improve everything but themselves off the face of the earth." And he adds, "I have no such passion for finding nothing but myself everywhere." Among our American writers a few, like Arnold, do not care to find only themselves everywhere, and these have told us a different story of the American Negro. They are poets and writers of fiction, men and women who are happy in meeting and appreciating different types of human beings.[1] If these writers were to instruct us, they would say that we must individualize more when we think of the black people about us, must differentiate. That, too, we must remember that when we pass judgment, we need to know whether our own standard is the best, whether we may

[1] Note especially the stories of Alice MacGowan and Grace MacGowan Cooke, and the poems of Rosalie M. Jonas.

not have something to learn from the stand-
ards of others. Supposing Ezekiel is delib-
erate and slow to make changes or to take
risks; are we who are "acceleration mad,"
who acquire heart disease hustling to catch
trains, who mortgate our farms to buy auto-
mobiles, who seek continually new sensa-
tions, really better than he? Is it not a
matter of difference, just as we may each
place in different order our desires, the one
choosing struggle for power and the accumulation of wealth, the other preferring serenity
and pleasure in the immediate present?
And lastly, after having praised our own
virtues and our own ideals, must we not
beware that we do not blame the Negro
when he adopts them, that we do not turn
upon him and fiercely demand only servile
virtues, the virtues that make him useful not
to himself but to us? [1]

[1] Careful readers of economic Negro studies by white
writers will notice this tendency to look upon the Negro as
belonging to a servile class. Emphasis is laid upon his responsibilities to the white man, not upon the white man's responsibilities to him. Any one familiar with the sympathetic
attitude toward the workers in such a study as the *Pittsburg
Survey* will notice at once the difference in attitude in Negro
surveys by whites, the slight emphasis laid upon the black

No one can talk for long of the Negro in America without propounding the all-embracing question, What will become of him, what will be the outcome of all this racial controversy? It is a daring person who attempts to answer. We, who have studied the Negro in New York, may perhaps venture to predict a little regarding his future in this city, his possible status in the later years of the century; whether he will lose in opportunity and social position, or whether he will advance in his struggle to be a man.

Looking upon the great population of the city, its varied races and nationalities, I confess that his outlook to me begins to be bright. New York is still to a quite remarkable extent dominated socially by its old American stock, its Dutch and Anglo-Saxon element. Few things strike the foreign visitor so forcibly as that despite its enormous European population, American society

laborers' long hours and poor pay, and the failure to emphasize the white man's responsibility. Negro laborers are still studied from the viewpoint of the capitalist. There is one notable exception to this, the study by the governor of Jamaica, Sir Sidney Olivier, on "White Capital and Coloured Labor."

is homogeneous. But this is not likely to continue for very long. When the present demand for exhausting self-supporting work becomes less insistent, we shall feel in a deeper, more vital way the influence of our vast foreign life. With a million Jews and nearly a million Latin peoples, we cannot for long be held in the provincialism of to-day. I suspect that to many Europeans New York seems still a great overgrown village in "a nation of villagers," pronouncing with narrow, dogmatic assurance upon the deep unsolved problems of life. But in the future it may take on a larger, more cosmopolitan spirit. Its Italians may bring a finer feeling for beauty and wholesome gayety, its Jews may continue to add great intellectual achievements, and its people of African descent, perhaps always few in number, may show with happy spontaneity their best and highest gifts. If New York really becomes a cosmopolitan city, let us believe the Negro will bring to it his highest genius and will walk through it simply, quietly, unnoticed, a man among men.

APPENDIX

THE federal census in 1900 contained a volume on the Negro in the United States, a source of information quoted by nearly every writer on the American Negro. The tables in that volume, however, do not classify by cities, and any one desiring information regarding the Negro in some especial city must search through other volumes. As this is a lengthy task, I am affixing a list of the tables in the census of 1900, treating of the Negro in New York City, believing that it may also be a guide to students of the new census of 1910, who wish to find New York Negro statistics.

Population. Vol. I, Part I. Published 1901.

Page 868, Table 57. Aggregate, white, and colored population distributed according to native or foreign parentage, for cities having 25,000 inhabitants or more: 1900.

Page 934, Table 81. Total males twenty-one years of age and over, classified by general nativity, color, and literacy, for cities having 25,000 inhabitants or more: 1900.

Vol. II. Published 1902.

Page 163, Table 19. Persons of school age, five to twenty years, inclusive, by general nativity and color, for cities having 25,000 inhabitants or more: 1900. Also, pages 165 and 167, Tables 20 and 21.

Page 332, Table 32. Conjugal condition of the aggregate population, classified by sex, general nativity, color, and age periods, for cities having 100,000 inhabitants or more: 1900.

Page 397, Table 54. Negro persons attending school during the census year, classified by sex and age periods, for cities having 25,000 inhabitants or more: 1900.

Page 737, Table 111. Persons owning and hiring their homes, classified by color, for cities having 100,000 inhabitants or more: 1900.

Vital Statistics. Vol. III. Published 1902.

Page 458, Table 19. Population, births, deaths, and death rates at certain ages, and deaths from certain causes, by sex, color, general nativity, and parent nativity: census year 1900.

Occupations. Published 1904.

Pages 634 to 642, Table 43. Total males and females, ten years of age and over, engaged in selected groups of occupations, classified by general nativity, color, conjugal condition, months unemployed, age periods, and parentage, for cities having 50,000 inhabitants or more: 1900.

Supplementary Analysis. Published 1906.

Page 262, Table 87. Per cent Negro in total population, 1900, 1890, and 1880, per cent male and female

APPENDIX 231

in Negro population, per cent illiterate in Negro population at least ten years of age, and among negro males of voting age, and per 10,000 distribution of Negro pupulation by age periods.

Women at Work. Published 1907.

Page 146, Table 9. Number and percentage of breadwinners in female population, sixteen years of age and over, classified by race and nativity, for cities having at least 50,000 inhabitants: 1900.

Pages 147 to 151, Table 10. Number and percentage of breadwinners in the female population, sixteen years and over, classified by age, race, and nativity.

Pages 266 to 275, Table 28. Female breadwinners, sixteen years of age and over, classified by family relationship, and by race, nativity, marital condition, and occupation, for selected cities: 1900.

Pages 354 to 365, Table 29. Female breadwinners, sixteen years of age and over, living at home, classified by the number of other breadwinners in the family, and by race, nativity, marital condition, and occupation, for selected cities: 1900.

Mortality Statistics. Published 1908.

Page 28. Number of deaths from all causes per 1,000 of population.

Page 376, Table 2. Deaths in each registration area, by age: 1908.

Pages 566 to 568, Table 8. Deaths in each city having 100,000 population or over in 1900, from certain causes and classes of causes, by age: 1908.

INDEX

Aldridge, Ira, 137.

Amalgamation, 168.

Andrews, Charles, civil rights of Negroes, 214.

Andrews, Chas. C., on education, 14; on industrial opportunity, 27.

Archer, William, 172.

Arnold, Matthew, 224.

Arthur, Chester A., 23.

Association for Improving the Condition of the Poor, 159.

Athens, Ga., 207.

Atlanta, Negroes in occupations in, 77, 91, 93; proportion of Negro women to men in, 148; suffrage in, 206.

Baker, Ray Stannard, on suffrage, 205.

Benefit societies, 175.

Birthplaces, 35.

Boese, Thomas, 15.

Brokers, real estate, 45, 108.

Brown, William, 14.

Bulkley, W. L., 161.

Burke v. Bosso, 215.

Burleigh, Harry, 126.

Businesses, 106–112.

Cahill, Marie, 133.

Charity Organization Society, 158.

Chesnutt, Charles W., 181.

Chesterton, Gilbert K., 222.

Churches: Baptist, 20, 116, 123; Catholic, 116; Congregational, 20; Episcopal, 20, 113, 116, 120; Methodist, 20, 116.

City and Suburban Homes, 41.

Civil rights: state bill, 213; violations of, 209, 210.

Clarkson, Thomas, 32.

Cleveland, Grover, 17.

Clinton, De Witt, 14.

Cole and Johnson, 127, 133.

Constitutional conventions, state, 11–13.

Cook, Will Marion, 136.

Cooke, Grace MacGowan, 224.

Court: children's, 66.
magistrate's, 202–204.